CREATIVE ACTIVITIES FOR THE EARLY YEARS

CREATIVE ACTIVITIES FOR THE EARLY YEARS

Stella Skinner

P·C·P

Paul Chapman
Publishing

© West Sussex County Council

First published 2007

Apart from any fair dealing for the purposes of research or
private study, or criticism or review, as permitted under the
Copyright, Designs and Patents Act, 1988, this publication
may be reproduced, stored or transmitted in any form, or by
any means, only with the prior permission in writing of the
publishers, or in the case of reprographic reproduction, in
accordance with the terms of licences issued by the Copyright
Licensing Agency. Enquiries concerning reproduction ouside
those terms should be sent to the publishers.

 Paul Chapman Publishing
A SAGE Publications Company
1 Oliver's Yard
55 City Road
London EC1Y 1SP

SAGE Publications Inc
2455 Teller Road
Thousand Oaks, California 91320

SAGE Publications India Pvt Ltd
B 1/I 1 Mohan Cooperative Industrial Area
Mathura Road, New Delhi 110 044
India

SAGE Publications Asia-Pacific Pte Ltd
33 Pekin Street #02-01
Far East Square
Singapore 048763

Library of Congress Control Number: 2007920334

A catalogue record for this book is available from the
British Library

ISBN 978-1-4129-3447-3
ISBN 978-1-4129-3448-0 (pbk)

Typeset by C&M Digitals (P) Ltd, Chennai, India
Printed in Great Britain by Cromwell Press Ltd, Trowbridge, Wiltshire
Printed on paper from sustainable resources

CONTENTS

AUTHOR'S ACKNOWLEDGEMENT

The author would like to extend her gratitude to her family for their patience and IT support, to her colleagues for their interest and enthusiasm and to her chauffeur for an impeccable service.

COMPANION WEBSITE

Go to: www.sagepub.co.uk/skinner

As an added resource, this book has a companion website. The site is packed with extra material to help you make your setting creative.

On the website, you can:

- Download blank activity planning sheets.

- See examples of completed planning sheets.

- Follow links to useful websites to help you access the best music, visual arts and dance sites.

- Look at lists of useful resources, to help you get started in your own setting.

- View Top Tips for your setting, that provide inspirational ideas for making your own instruments, and ideas for working with different types of art materials.

You will also see photos of children in a variety of early years settings putting these activities into practice. Finally, a list of books you might like directs you to other texts that may be of interest to you and your setting.

THE CREATABILITY PROJECT

In the spring of 2005 two visual artists developed a programme of weekly sessions for five nursery settings in West Sussex. These sessions formed the basis of the pilot project and consisted of introducing children and practitioners to a wide variety of visual arts processes and materials. The intention was to raise the profile of creativity in the early years by offering the opportunity for practitioners to work alongside practising artists and by involving the families as much as possible. In this way, working from a largely child-led activity, the adults were encouraged to observe and reflect on the child's developing skills and the children were encouraged to discover how the tools and materials worked.

Following the success of the pilot project it was decided that a wider range of artists would work together offering opportunities to develop and integrate the visual arts, music and dance. The approach of the CreatAbility project to working with Early Years can be summarised as follows:

- To encourage children to lead their own exploration of the materials or processes.
- To encourage children to work collaboratively.
- To stimulate creative thinking skills and problem solving solutions.
- To focus on process rather than product.
- To use skills, materials and processes that are easily transferable to staff and parents.
- To demonstrate ways of recording the children's experiences.
- To use materials that are easily available.
- To consider the environments and routines when planning the workshops.

Ten settings in West Sussex were selected to take part in the next phase of the project. In March 2006 four lead artists and three local artists visited the settings to meet the practitioners, to see what spaces were available to use and to ensure that staff understood the ethos of the workshops that were going to take place. The artists decided to use the theme of journeys as a starting point to describe the experiential journey the children would take, moving from one art form to another in a variety of spaces.

The project took place over 8 weeks in the summer of 2006 and the evaluations were very positive, with many practitioners recognising that they needed to allow far more time for children to experiment with materials. They were also impressed with the way the children developed in confidence and asked more probing questions about the process that was being explored. The project gave practitioners the opportunity to observe the children working with other adults and to consider their own practice and training needs.

Acknowledgements

The whole team would like to thank the children and staff at the following settings for their enthusiasm and commitment:

Bognor Regis Nursery School
Glade Nursery, Bognor Regis
Kingston Bucci First School, Shoreham-by-Sea
Little Owls Nursery, Hawthorns First School, Durrington
Magic Minders Worthing Childminders Association, Worthing
Manor Green Primary School, Crawley
Play Centre Nursery, Wickbourne Centre, Littlehampton
Stepping Stones Neighbourhood Nursery, Bognor Regis
Westerfields Day Nursery, Worthing
Woodstock Day Nursery, Worthing

Also:
The CreatAbility Project was devised and managed by West Sussex County Council's Arts Service and was generously supported by Arts Council England South East and West Sussex County Council. Thanks also to the members of staff in the Early Childhood Service, Children and Young People's Services, Bognor Regis Nursery School and Family Learning, whose advice and support has been invaluable.

The CreatAbility team consisted of:

Visual artists
Claire Simpson   Claire studied on a Foundation Course at Lincoln Art College and then took a degree in Fine Art at Bretton Hall, Leeds University. She currently works as an artist, project facilitator and trainer, working with people of all ages through her collaboration with organisations and community groups. www. axisweb.org

Teresa Grimaldi   Teresa trained in theatre design and puppetry at Central School of Speech and Drama and has recently completed an MA in Visual performance at Dartington College of Arts. She is a practising visual artist developing installation and puppetry ideas that are enriched by her work with early years children.

Jane Chalk   Jane studied at the University of Plymouth gaining a BA Hons in 3D Design. She creates costumes and stage props for theatre, film and carnival and is also a Level Three qualified playworker working with children in many different environments, exploring materials and found objects to create wonderful and imaginative costumes, puppets and masks.

Musicians

Sharon Quinn   Sharon grew up in West Africa, developing a love of African music. She combined studying early vocal music at Kingston University, Surrey, gaining a BEd Hons, with performing electronic music. She has worked in Britain, Western and Eastern Europe, teaching, singing and collaborating with other artists and children.

Louise Bradbury   Louise studied at the Royal Academy of Music and teaches recorder at the Guildhall School of Music and Drama Junior School. She works as a freelance musician and has established the pre-school music programme, *little notes for little folks,* currently serving over 200 families in Horsham, West Sussex. www.littlenotesforlittlefolks.co.uk

Dance artists

Amanda Drago   Amanda trained at the Laban Centre, London and the Northern School of Contemporary Dance, Leeds. She performed in dance and theatre companies for many years and in 2004 started her own dance company, called Falling Cat. Her first work, 'Closer', is a sensory movement installation for children with autistic spectrum disorders.

Natasha McKenzie   Natasha began her career as a nursery assistant and then took a degree in Dance and Women's Studies at Roehampton University. She has worked with experimental and professional dance companies and has been a 'stand in' in films and pop videos. She runs youth dance workshops in Sussex and London.

Photographer

Matthew Andrews   Matthew trained at St Martins School of Art in London and has worked as a photographer for 14 years specialising in arts and education. Recent assignments include the Sultan's Elephant and Urban Cultural programme for Arts Council England and the Brighton Festival, which he photographs each year in May. www.matthewandrews.co.uk

The book has been written to support and develop the ethos of the CreatAbility project and to demonstrate to practitioners ways in which they could apply ideas and activities to their own settings, with the emphasis being on the concept of offering a creative learning experience rather than a 'doing activity'. The book also demonstrates ways in which the creative arts can be integrated, as this is something that young children do naturally. The creative activities described include the visual arts, music and movement and dance, and are illustrated and supported by photographs.

Chapter 1 describes the importance of the creative arts and suggests ways in which practitioners might consider their own setting with a view to developing this area of learning.

Chapters 2 to 4, Starting from Visual Art, Starting from Music and, Starting from Movement and Dance, describe the importance of each of the creative art forms, including ideas that might support a less confident practitioner. The chapters are then divided into two sections, each giving three examples of how one creative arts activity can lead into other creative art forms taking ideas from the children and practitioners. The examples given combine stage-by-stage instructions of the exploration process alongside descriptions of what happened when we explored the activity with children during the project.

Practitioners may like to follow the illustrated theme but are also encouraged to use the ideas described and personalise them to suit the needs of the children in their setting. It is most likely that even when using the given structure to the session, different children will take the exploration in another direction. The suggested activities may be used singly or as part of a set, and when considering the suitability of an activity for an individual setting, practitioners are advised to consider the following points:

- The size of the group they are going to work with and whether extra adults will be needed to support the children.

- The age range within the group.

- Available space and how long it will stay available.

- Will the activity need adapting for any children with specific learning needs?

- The illustrated activity does not all have to take place in one session – it may suit the needs of a setting better to split it up over several days and examples have been divided into stages to assist the practitioner if this is the case.

The example of each activity is described in terms of a standard planning format, described below, in which are inserted descriptions of what might be included under each heading. A photocopiable example of the blank format is included here and can also be downloaded from the companion website. The examples of creative arts activities in the following chapters illustrate the process that was explored during the project; therefore the detail on why the activity was chosen and the opportunities for differentiation are specific to particular groups and will obviously vary according to individual settings.

ACTIVITY PLAN

Theme:
This could be a general theme that the setting is investigating for a period of time or an abstract idea to develop, for example 'journeys'.

Creative arts activity:
A brief description of the process that is going to be explored.

Why?
The activity may be a result of the children's interest, an observation of a child at play, or the decision that certain skills are not being fully explored. It really makes a difference to the quality of the activity if all practitioners understand exactly why this activity is being made available to the children.

Possible learning outcomes: The children might:		Questions to ask:
Health and safety considerations:	Theme: / Creative arts activity: / Why:	Opportunities for differentiation:
Resources:		Relevant Curriculum links:

Suggested resources:
The resources available for the children to use are described, with alternatives if appropriate. Practitioners should be aware that children may also suggest or find their own resources.

Suggested questions to ask:
These are some ideas to get the children thinking and responding, which will enable the children to take the activity forward.

Possible learning outcomes:
These will be linked to the 'development matters' stages of the creative area of learning leading towards the early learning goal for the creative area of learning. The term 'possible' is used because the children may develop the activity in ways the practitioner had not considered.

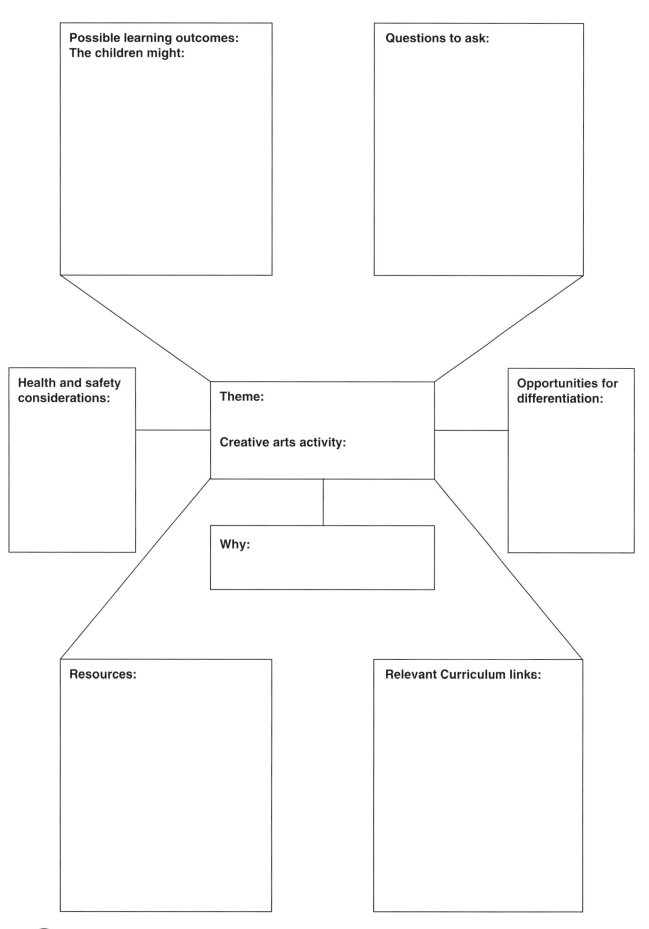

Possible learning outcomes:
The children might:

Questions to ask:

Health and safety
considerations:

Theme:

Creative arts activity:

Opportunities for
differentiation:

Why:

Resources:

Relevant Curriculum links:

Opportunities for differentiation:
These will indicate an understanding of the different learning styles within the group and ways in which the activity may need to be adapted.

Relevant curriculum links:
Creative arts activities can link to all the other areas of learning and resources should be available to support these connections. The children, during the exploration process, may also make some unexpected links. The described activities mainly include a reference to MD (Mathematical Development, which will be called Problem Solving, Reasoning and Numeracy), CLL (Communication, Language and Literacy) and KUW (Knowledge and Understanding of the World).

Health and safety considerations:
Any potential risks attached to the activity are identified.

Each activity is further described under the following three headings:

Exploration process   This describes the stages that the exploration process could be expected to take. Practitioners are reminded that their children may well discover a different direction to go in and that is all part of the creative experience. The examples in the book describe the journey we took with the children in our sessions. In some cases we have included comments from children as an indication of their involvement.

Assessment opportunities   Ways in which the children's involvement and progress could be recorded.

Ways forward   This forms an evaluation of the activity, which, based on the children's response may clearly indicate a way forward that the practitioner can plan for.

It is not intended that practitioners should feel they have to use this planning format for every creative activity as that would be completely impractical. However, if a setting is interested in developing its approach to the creative arts it would be a worthwhile exercise to do at regular intervals, thereby ensuring that practitioners are confident about the reason for and the quality of the creative experiences the children are being offered.

Also included as an Appendix is a format for recording the way in which the creative arts projects within a setting are linking together. An example format is included for each of the 18 sets of activities in Chapters 2–4, as well as a blank photocopiable version. Practitioners may also download the format from the companion website.

The book concludes with a list of *Resources*, including details of materials, suppliers and some further reading suggestions from the artists.

CHAPTER 1

An approach to creative learning in the early years

This chapter will give you ideas to consider concerning:

- The importance of developing creative activities in the early years.
- Developing an ethos and structure to support creative activities.
- Further reading.

Creativity is about representing one's own image, not reproducing someone else's. (B. Duffy, *Supporting Creativity and Imagination in the Early Years*, p.10)

Figure 1.1   This little boy explored a whole range of creative activities via his senses, culminating in the observation of the shadow of his hand in the water tray

The importance of developing creative skills

We have the evidence in archaeological remains and historical artefacts that humans have always commented on the world they live in, using available materials as well as their voices and bodies to record stories, songs and dance. The need to describe and share experiences seems to be very important to us. Studies of child development have revealed that children must have the opportunity to produce representations that reflect their own experiences, thoughts and feelings. Offering young children the opportunity to explore a rich range of creative experiences will help to develop a child who is able to:

- Make connections with others by 'speaking' feelings in verbal/non-verbal ways.

- Express thoughts and possibilities on a given subject.

- Challenge ideas and problem solve in a variety of situations.

- Develop a personal definition of aesthetic beauty.

- Consider cultural issues.

- Demonstrate good self-esteem.

- Extend physical skills.

These are life skills that will enable young children not only to access all areas of learning but to develop their full potential as human beings.

How does creative development feature in the Early Years curriculum?

At the time of writing, the curriculum guidance for Early Years is undergoing a revision with the intention to bring together, in 2008, the Birth to Three Matters framework with the QCA Curriculum Guidance for the Foundation Stage to create an Early Years Foundation Stage framework for services to children from birth to five.

The Early Years Foundation Stage framework for services to children from birth to five has Creative Development as one of its six areas of learning and development, dividing it into four concepts:

- Being creative – responding to experiences and expressing and communicating ideas.

- Exploring media and materials – 2D and 3D representations.

- Creating music and dance.

- Developing imagination and imaginative play.

Each concept describes the pathway that the children's progress might take, illustrated by the 'development matters' section in the framework guidance, culminating in the Early Learning Goal which most children should achieve by the end of their Reception year.

Early Years practitioners will be aware of what a huge area of learning this is and how many important connections it can make to the other five areas of learning and development.

If a setting cultivates a creative approach to any area of learning, the practitioners will be encouraging children to:

- Have the confidence to air new ideas and develop them as far as possible.

- Learn from past experiences and relate this learning to new situations.

- Invent individual methods of problem solving.

- Create something that is unique and original.

Current research which supports this approach to learning

The ethos of the **CreatAbility Project** has been heavily influenced by the interesting results emerging from the Reggio Emilia approach to pre-school education in Italy. In essence, the young child is considered to be already capable, strong, possessing curiosity and the ability to construct his/her own learning. The importance of the child's collaborative skills and relationships with family, peers and community is given a high profile. The children are stimulated to communicate in many different forms, such as symbolic representation, word, movement, building, sculpture, dramatic play, shadow play, music. The environment the child plays in is considered to be the third teacher, with much thought being given to the use of space and light. The practitioners take the role of partner, nurturer, friend and facilitator of the children's exploration of themes. (See further reading suggestions.)

This approach is further supported by the **Effective Provision of Pre-School Education (EPPE)** report, which focused on the effectiveness of Early Years education and was able to identify elements of effective practice, including the importance of the quality of the adult–child verbal interactions and the balance of child- and adult-initiated activity. An environment in which play was valued alongside new skills being introduced was seen to be very beneficial to the child, as was the active engagement of parents in their children's learning.

Thirdly, the Government's Green Paper *Every Child Matters*, produced in 2003, outlined five outcomes for children, one of which was that children should be able to enjoy and achieve. This has had a big impact on the quality of children's learning, particularly in the way in which children's views are being taken into account and developed.

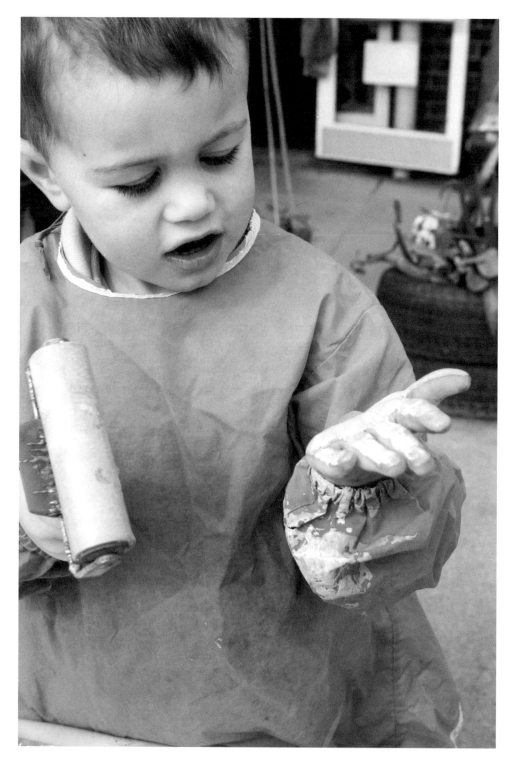

Figure 1.2   A monoprinting session which entailed much more than just making a print

Definition of Early Years

The focus of the book is about working with children in the Foundation Stage (3–5) range, although some of the ideas could easily be adapted to suit the needs of older or younger children. In terms of curriculum planning the book refers to possible learning outcomes relating to the appropriate Creative Early Learning Goals and potential links to other areas of the curriculum.

What do we need in place to support an imaginative delivery of the creative arts?

This section will look at factors that will support the planning and delivery of the creative area of learning and give the practitioner some questions to consider within individual settings.

The ethos of the setting

Process over product

Observations of children at play clearly reveal that young children are fascinated by the exploration of materials and tools and we know that children learn as much from the 'doing' as from the potential end product. Figure 1.2 illustrates the child's fascination with the experience of using paint and a roller. The planned creative activity was to explore mono-printing but practitioners were amazed at how long some children spent investigating the properties of the materials and using them in unexpected ways. This illustrates that the sensitive interaction between the child and practitioner is an important part of this discovery process and it is not just a question of the adult standing back and supervising the activity. The child will be watching the practitioner's reaction to their investigation and needing reassurance that they are not doing something wrong. If there is an end product, and sometimes there has to be, it should be unique and meaningful to the child. The understanding of this ethos should be clear and carried out positively throughout the setting.

Routines

Young children really need the time to play, to discover the possibilities and potential of the world around them. If this time is given sparingly within the confines of too rigid a routine, the learning outcomes for the child will be limited. This has big implications for planning because practitioners need to ensure that there have been planned opportunities for children simply to explore materials before a specific skills activity takes place. Settings also need to consider their daily structures and observe whether, as far as possible, these allow for freedom of exploration. If this exploration is facilitated in a sensitive way with a balance of adult-led and child-initiated play and the opportunity to return to an activity, the children's emotional and communication skills will flourish and the practitioner will be able to observe a wealth of important steps in the child's development.

Points to consider

1. Do we have an agreed ethos within our setting, which describes the way in which creative learning will be facilitated? Do all practitioners understand and deliver it or is further training needed?
2. If we offer flexible sessions are we sure that all children can access a wide and varied range of activities?
3. Does our daily routine allow time for children to explore materials? Are there opportunities for children to revisit an experience?
4. Does our assessment process complement the learning which is taking place through play?
5. Are the children currently producing their own unique creations?

The learning environment (inside and outside)

Physical space

Whatever the type of setting, this should be maximised to allow real potential for exploration and creativity. Young children naturally move about a great deal when taking part in activities, operating at different levels, and consideration needs to be given to the arrangement of the furniture and flexibility of its use. An easy way to assess this is to make a series of tracking observations of the children to see which areas of the learning environment are being used and which are being ignored. Observations of the children's learning styles will also support any decision to rearrange an area. Involving the children in this decision is really useful and offers them the opportunity to express their views and to realise that their opinions will be listened to and acted on. Many settings have made 'before and after' books illustrating the changes they have made to an area of their learning environment.

Some settings are now considering the effects of different lighting on children and are experimenting with lower levels of light in some rooms. When planning a creative activity it is important to think about the space that is going to be used and whether the available lighting will affect the children's participation in and understanding of the activity. For example, if you want the children to really observe the fine detail in a natural object, such as a shell, the activity needs to take place in a well-lit area and not on a small dark table well away from the window. Colours are very affected by light and for children to appreciate the vibrancy of the colour they might be mixing it is essential that the available light is good. Most activities planned for young children can take place either inside or outside and many of the examples in the book happened in the outside environment. There are many arguments for children to have the availability of an outside space, one of which is that children have the opportunity to really explore and expand an activity when they are outside and practitioners often feel more relaxed in a less constricted space. The outside space does not have to be huge,

Figure 1.3   By the simple hanging of items on a bush, an outdoor area suddenly offers more possibilities

but can be imaginatively set up, as shown in Figure 1.3 in which objects have been displayed on a bush to stimulate the children's imagination. In the same way as young children often like small, cosy areas indoors, it is possible to offer them similar opportunities outside with the use of draped materials, small tents and builders' trays with an assortment of natural objects to explore, such as shells and pebbles.

It would be ideal if children were able to have free access to both indoor and outdoor spaces for a significant part of their session.

Organisation

The organisation of the indoor and outdoor space needs to be logically planned to ensure that children can access what they need easily and staff can locate appropriate resources when setting up an area. A well-organised learning environment, such as the area illustrated by Figure 1.4, encourages independent learning and supports a child who may need to access materials to develop an idea. The involvement of the children in the arrangement of the learning environment is recommended as it helps them to identify the resources that are available and to make their own suggestions about what they might like.

The organisation of the resources is equally important so that all children, whatever their level of development, can access equipment. Containers should be clearly labelled with words and/or pictures, and resources such as glue and

Figure 1.4   Well-organised resources support children's ability to select the piece of equipment they think they might need for the task ahead

scissors should always have a base to which they can be returned. Many resources will 'travel' round a setting and practitioners should agree that in a creative learning environment children would need to have the freedom to experiment with resources. Of course, there may need to be ground rules about clearing-up time.

Resources

It is important that children are offered a wide variety of resources, many of which can be obtained very cheaply, because these will contribute to a broad and balanced curriculum. It is also necessary for practitioners to appreciate that different media will allow children to address problems and explore materials in different ways. For example, items such as large plastic magnifying mirrors which are easy to grasp can be used for a variety of activities. Figure 1 on the companion website illustrates a starting point for an exploration of colour. The children had been mark-making on paper and the little girl realised she had inadvertently got colour on her nose! She was fascinated by her reflection in the mirror, which she then used all around the learning environment to look for different colours.

These resources should reflect a range of different cultures and social structures to ensure that all children feel represented in their learning environment. Families are usually very willing to contribute resources once they know what would be useful and if they are able to see it being used – for example, an

Figure 1.5   A builder's tray (mixing spot) filled with natural objects provides a starting point for an exploration of printmaking

interactive display of children's printmaking inspired by beautiful textiles which their families have contributed. It is really important that resources are sorted regularly, well maintained and removed if they appear too shabby, as children deserve access to high quality materials. An essential and easy resource to build up, as shown in Figure 1.5 would be an extensive range of natural objects, for example shells, stones, pieces of wood, all of which can provide a stimulating start to an activity. Each creative arts activity example in the book suggests resources that might be used, and at the end of the book is a list of useful resources which a setting could build on.

Displays

Visually, the environment that the children play in should be stimulating to encourage curiosity. Displays need to be at an appropriate level for the children so that they can see and respond to them and can also include items to encourage interaction. It is important that displays reflect a wide range of cultures, incorporating materials, pictures, photographs and music. They should celebrate individuality and could illustrate the wide range of activities that take place in the setting, as shown in Figure 2 on the companion website, thus ensuring that the families feel well informed and included in the learning process. Many parents and carers are unable, due to work commitments, to spend much quality time in their child's setting, so these displays will make a big difference to their knowledge about the experiences their child is having on a daily basis.

Displays of children's work should represent all the children and could show the process of the activity, supported by photographs and children's comments, as much as the finished piece. It is important that displays are well maintained, beautifully presented and changed regularly, because if practitioners have stopped noticing the displays then the children certainly have.

Points to consider

1. Does the indoor space layout make sense – if not, how can we improve it? Have we asked the children what they think? Have we then told parents about the process?
2. Do we really need all the furniture? Do we offer activities at different levels?
3. Consider the outside provision opportunities. What do we like and what else would we like? How do practitioners feel about being outside?
4. Do all areas look stimulating and inviting. Would you like to play here?
5. Can the children access the resources independently and does everyone know where resources are stored?
6. Are the resources stimulating? Are they in good condition? Do they reflect a wide range of different cultures?
7. Do the displays reflect the many activities that are taking place daily?
8. Do the displays inform families about the value placed on their child's contribution to the setting?

The role of the practitioner

Attitude

Practitioners working with young children set the scene for the emotional environment that the children play in. It is important that they are able to represent a secure world in which the children are encouraged to take risks knowing that they will be supported if necessary, as demonstrated by the practitioner in Figure 1.6. The little girl was not sure how she felt about being asked to lie down on the material but there was a grown-up beside her demonstrating that it would be fine. The value that the practitioners place on creativity will be recognised by the children, who are constantly watching their reactions and picking up on often very subtle body language. Each practitioner really needs to 'know' the children so that through sensitive observation he or she will know when to intervene, when to extend, when to keep out. Ideally the practitioner should frequently play alongside the child, demonstrating that he or she also has things to find out about the materials and tools.

Training

It is important that practitioners understand the process and potential development of a creative activity so they are prepared to support the child. This can only

Figure 1.6   Staff are actively involved in the exploration process and the girl is reassured that it is safe to lie down on the material

happen if they have tried it out themselves. If the preparation is inadequate the practitioner will lose confidence and the session will turn into an instruction. They need to develop the skills that enable them to have valuable conversations with the child and to appreciate the importance of observing, recording and reflecting on the child's development. This training can take place in a variety of ways, either formally through courses, in the setting as part of a specific in-house interest in developing an area of learning or often simply through one member of staff having a particular interest or enthusiasm for a creative activity and passing this on to colleagues.

Reflection

A reflective practitioner will appreciate the necessity to ensure that all children are given equal opportunities to explore an idea and this could involve adapting and expanding activities. It might also sometimes be necessary to challenge one's own prejudices when delivering the curriculum. For example, it is very easy to avoid planning, usually quite subconsciously, for an activity that we personally do not enjoy doing. Examples of this could be cooking food that we personally don't like or playing with the clay if we personally don't like the feel of it on our hands.

Points to consider

1. Are we agreed about what we mean by the word 'creative'?
2. Do we find out about or try out the process of the creative activity before we introduce it to the children? Do we play alongside the children often enough? This means in a range of situations such as child-initiated play as well as an adult-focused activity.
3. Are we sure that we are not allowing any prejudices we may have, for example not liking the feel of clay, or the taste of a particular food, to influence the children?
4. Can we identify any training needs?

The role of the family

Communication

The communication between practitioners and parents/carers will play a vital role in supporting a creative environment. Parents have the right to be informed about activities that their child is being offered and are often very willing to be involved in the activity themselves. Good communication between the setting and family ensures that the ethos of the setting is clearly understood and there will be no confusion about work in the form of Mother's Day cards, daily paintings or drawings that are or are not coming home. This communication will take place naturally via home visits and open sessions where the families are invited in to play alongside the children, as illustrated by Figure 1.7. This was a brilliant opportunity for parents to really understand what opportunities were being offered to their child during a nursery session and the children loved showing off their skills and knowledge about tools and materials to their family. It is also evident from the result of asking parents their views about settings that newsletters, displays and the day-to-day conversations are very important to them.

Relationship

The interrelationship between the child, the family and setting will inevitably play a large part in the child's creative development as the child will bring into the setting their home and past experiences, incorporating them into methods of exploration. The way in which the practitioners perceive and discuss these with the family will support the child. The family can offer a wealth of creative expertise, contributing to the richness of the offered curriculum.

Points to consider

1. How comfortable do other adults feel in the setting? How do we know?
2. How involved do adults become in their child's learning? Would we like to develop this involvement?
3. How do we show that we value each child's/family's contribution to the setting?

Figure 1.7   This little boy loves having his dad alongside him, helping to make a dinosour at his Nursery open day

An inclusive environment

Every child has the right to rest and leisure, to engage in play and recreational activities appropriate to the age of the child and to participate freely in cultural life and the arts. (Article 31 United Nations Convention on the Rights of the Child)

Entitlement

We all have an entitlement to reach our full potential and the seeds of this are sown in our early years at home and in pre-school settings. Practitioners must ensure, through careful planning and evaluation, that all children feel special and are given the best possible opportunities to develop their potential.

Planning

A well-planned, quality creative experience will encourage children to use all their senses, as illustrated by Figure 1.8, so that an activity that includes a child who has specific learning needs can be adapted and expanded. Adopting an open-ended approach to the learning experience facilitates planning but practitioners are advised to seek specialist help if necessary to ensure they are exploring all possibilities for that child. The (draft) Early Years Foundation Stage Framework (DfES, 2006) states that there should be:

Figure 1.8   Staff adapted the available space and adult support to make sure that all children, whatever their needs, were included in the musical exploration

Opportunities for children with visual impairment to access and have physical contact with artefacts, materials, spaces and movement.

Opportunities for children with hearing impairment to experience sound and physical contact with instruments and other sources of sound.

Opportunities for children who cannot communicate by voice to respond to music in different ways, such as gestures.

Figure 3 on the companion website illustrates a group of children exploring a range of instruments, which is an activity that takes place daily in many settings. The learning intentions were the same for these children with specific learning needs as for any other children but the activities are being adapted by the practitioners to support their individual stages of development. In any setting it is important that the exploration of a creative arts activity will be available to all children and it is the task of the practitioner to adapt the activity as appropriate to the needs of the child. Activities described in the following chapters included children with a wide range of physical and behavioural needs.

Equal opportunities

All races, religions, cultures and genders must be valued and given equal status in the curriculum via stories, displays, music, dance, resources, visitors and outside visits. It will probably be necessary to audit resources regularly to ensure that all possibilities have been considered, for example family structure, and practitioners should be aware of new publications and resources which they might like to buy to support what the setting offers.The Early Years Foundation Stage Framework (DfES, 2006) advises that to give all children the best opportunity for effective creative development, practitioners should give attention to 'accommodating children's specific religious or cultural beliefs relating to particular forms of art or methods of expression'.

Points to consider

1. What evidence do we have that the setting values each individual child?
2. Would an audit of our resources reveal any gaps that need filling?
3. Are we sure we include opportunities for differentiation in our planning?
4. Would observations reveal any gender issues that might need tackling?
5. Do we know whom to contact for advice if we have a child with specific learning difficulties?

FURTHER READING

Duffy, B. (1998) *Supporting Creativity and Imagination in the Early Years*. Buckingham: Open University Press.

Bruce, T. (2004) *Cultivating Creativity in Babies, Toddlers and Young Children*. London: Hodder & Stoughton.

Edwards, C., Gandini, L. and Forman, G. (eds) (1993) *The Hundred Languages of Children: The Reggio Emilia Approach to Early Childhood Education*. Norwood, NJ: Ablex.

HM Government (2003) *Every Child Matters*. Cm 5860. London: The Stationery office.

Other resources

DfES (2004) *Every Child Matters: Change for Children*. www.everychildmatters.gov.uk/ publications

DfES/Institute of London, University of London. (2005) *Effective Provision of Pre-School Education (EPPE) Project*. www.ioe.ac.uk/schools/ecpe/eppe/

DfES (2006) *The Early Years Foundation Stage* (draft). www.standards.dfes.gov.uk/ primary/foundation_stage_practitioners/

HM Government (2004) *Every Child Matters: Change for Children*. www.everychildmatters. gov.uk/publications/

Further information on projects and publications of interest to Early Years practitioners can be found on the Department for Education and Skills (DfES) website: www.dfes/gov/uk

Starting from the visual arts

This chapter will give you ideas of ways to develop the visual arts by:

- Highlighting the importance of the visual arts.
- Offering practical solutions to common concerns.
- Illustrating two visual art activities each leading to an exploration of dance and music.

Exposure to the visual arts offers children the opportunity to explore the possibilities of two-dimensional and three-dimensional representations. If they are offered a wide range of activities and encouraged to use all their senses, children will be stimulated to express their emotions and ideas in a variety of ways. They will be given the opportunity to explore and begin to make sense of the world they live in and make connections in their life experiences.

Hopefully they will feel confident enough to take risks and try something new. In adult life most important discoveries have been initiated by creative risk-taking and it is important that we value this skill.

To summarise, the visual arts play an important role in developing creative awareness in young children in the following ways:

- Children are enabled to express their feelings and thoughts in non-verbal ways.

- Children are encouraged to challenge perceptions through developing unique creations.

- Children develop an appreciation of beauty and what that can mean to each individual person. This includes the observation of artists' work and the chance to work alongside artists.

- Children are presented with opportunities to solve problems imaginatively.

■ Children's self-esteem is nurtured as their peers and adults observe and support their ideas.

■ Children have opportunities to explore and celebrate a wide range of cultural differences.

■ Children have opportunities to investigate a wide range of materials.

Examples of **two-dimensional exploration** include:

■ Mark-making with a range of tools using fine and gross motor skills.

■ Painting with a wide variety of paints and tools.

■ Finger painting.

■ Printmaking.

Examples of **three-dimensional exploration** include:

■ Opportunities to use all senses to explore a variety of objects, including natural and made objects from a range of cultures.

■ The chance to make structures of a chosen scale using an assortment of materials some of which will be new and demand new skills.

■ The exploration of malleable materials such as clay, playdough and paint mixed with other substances, for example sawdust or glue.

■ Most settings include visual art activities in their daily planning because they are always popular with the children and link well with all areas of learning in the curriculum. However there can be the danger of not providing a wide enough range of experiences which results in the children and practitioners becoming demotivated. There are also issues around the provision of visual arts, which can deter practitioners from considering many options. The following points may provide some support and reassure a reluctant practitioner.

! DON'T PANIC IF...

We haven't got enough space to really explore an art activity.
Review the amount of furniture currently in the room, as settings often have too much. Don't forget to make good use of any outside space and don't disregard using floor space and wall space, because young children like to work at different levels.

We don't have access to water.
Make a fuss, because this is a basic requirement in an Early Years setting. You need access to a sink, and ideally one that is not also used for food preparation. Also the children need to be able to wash their

hands independently but you could use a bucket of warm water for this if you don't want them trailing paint across a room.

I'm worried about the activity making a big mess.

Young children cannot fully explore the possibilities of an activity if they are worried about making a mess. However, there is such a thing as damage limitation. You can protect surfaces with plastic cloths – plain shower curtains are ideal. Many settings use highly coloured, patterned cloths, which make it very difficult for children to focus on the art activity, as the background is so distractive. Practitioners need to operate as a team to set up, support and clear up, often with the children's help, a creative activity. Also, if you are lucky enough to have a separate space for creative activities don't call it the 'messy room' as it sends out a very negative view about art activities to children, parents and practitioners.

Our parents complain if their child gets in a mess.

Even wearing old clothes or aprons will not prevent children getting paint or glue on their clothes or hair and many settings find that the children can be quite hampered by some types of protective clothing. The setting should have a policy to explain that the children will be offered experiences that may leave their mark on clothes and parents need to appreciate the necessity for this in terms of child development.

Our parents want to receive an 'end result' from creative activities.

Sometimes they will see an end result, but you need to explain why it won't be every time. However, you can take photos of an exploration process and display these to share the experience with families. Another idea is to tie a luggage label to a child's bag with 'ask me about' written on it and a few words to jog the child's memory about the activity.

I feel that our creative activities are rushed and mass produced.

If you have an open-ended approach to the process then you won't know what you are going to produce so the children could potentially all do something different. In terms of time, you need to consider the setting's routines and ensure that each child does have the opportunity to fully explore a process. You could think about providing a creative activity, possibly with variations, over several days to accommodate those children who like to return to activities and explore them further as well as the children who do not attend regular sessions.

We don't have a big budget for lots of resources.

A letter sent out to families with a list of the kinds of items you could use will nearly always be productive but make sure you have adequate storage facilities. You do not have to buy products from educational suppliers – many of the resources used on the project were bought very cheaply from stores and 'pound shops', but remember to consider any health and safety issues. There is a list of resources and possible suppliers at the end of the book.

I find myself running out of ideas.

Although working from a theme can lend a structure to the planning, sometimes it helps to start from a more abstract idea such as journeys, pattern or colour because these are more conducive to exploration and tend to have a less prescriptive outcome. Listening to the children and following their lead will give you new ideas as will having artists into the setting to work with the children. There are many television programmes, websites and books that could suggest ideas, which you can always adapt to suit the needs of your setting.

I'm not sure how much help to give the children.
Your interest in their exploration is the best help you can give, as well as working alongside them to demonstrate that you too have things to find out about the process. Make sure that any tools they are provided with, such as scissors, really work properly. Our artists placed lengths of pre-cut sticky tape on a plastic cutting board so the children could peel them off when needed. Give the child time to attempt a task and then ask if he or she would like some help, ensuring that they assist you in some way, even if it's by holding the tape.

I'm worried it might get chaotic.
It is fine to restrict the size of the group, reassuring other children that there will be plenty of time for them to play later. In this way you are ensuring a quality experience for children and practitioners. It works well to introduce equipment gradually during an exploration process rather than having it all available from the start. You will also have basic ground rules about behaviour and respect for equipment that still apply, even though it is a creative exploration.

The following two sections demonstrate ways in which visual art activities could lead into an exploration of other creative art forms.

Example activities starting from the visual arts (1)

Example 2A   Visual art activity

ACTIVITY PLAN

Theme:
▶ Pathways.

Creative arts activity:
▶ Exploration of materials.

Why?
▶ To provide children with an opportunity to direct their own learning from a variety of experiences.

Suggested resources:
▶ Large space, which could be in a hall or outside.
▶ Large parachute or material hooked up and pegged out to make a big tent.
▶ Plain paper taped to floor inside tent with mark-making tools.

Possible learning outcomes: The children might:

Questions to ask:

Health and safety considerations:

Theme:

Creative arts activity:

Opportunities for differentiation:

Why:

Resources:

Relevant Curriculum links:

▸ Four small 'pop-up' tents or enclosed areas with mini scenarios set up inside each one. The ones we used are described fully in the exploration process.

▸ Assortment of widths of coloured tape stuck to the floor and leading to all the tents from a variety of directions.

▸ Small world equipment, cars, animals.

▸ Gaffer tape, pre-cut.

▸ Small rolls of paper, for example till rolls.

▸ A selection of bendy tent poles.

▸ A selection of strips of materials.

▸ An assortment of empty boxes, string, wool, card, paper etc.

Suggested questions to ask:

▸ What do we use pathways for?

▸ Where do you think they might take you?

▸ What do you think you will see on the way?

Possible learning outcomes:

The children might:

▸ Capture experiences and responses with paint and other materials or words.

▸ Talk about personal intentions, describing what they were trying to do.

▸ Create three-dimensional structures.

▸ Understand that different media can be combined to create new effects.

Opportunities for differentiation:

▸ Adult support – will really enhance these activities.

▸ A wide range of different sizes and types of tools.

Relevant curriculum links:

▸ CLL – making up a story; producing a record of the exploration.

▸ KUW – designing and making; time and place.

Health and safety considerations:

▸ Use of tent poles.

▸ Tent taped to floor.

Exploration process

The space will have been previously set up with all resources in place.

Stage one – introduce the theme

1. Invite the children to sit in a circle at the edge of the room. They will already be curious about what is happening in the space around them. Roll a narrow length of paper across the circle and ask the children what it looks like. Our children instantly said 'a road, a line, a path'. Taking the children's suggestions, extend

their vocabulary a little by asking where the pathway might lead to? Perhaps to the park or the beach. Ask the children what might they see on the way if they were to follow the path? This session should not last for too long because the children will want to get exploring the exciting scenario you have set up.

2. Explain that they are going to follow the tape pathways on the floor and see where they lead to. They can follow whichever path they like and do not all have to go together. The next stage describes the activities we presented but any adaptations to suit individual resources would work. The length of this session is dependent on the developmental stage of the children and the amount of available adult support at each area. This is a great opportunity to observe different learning styles so ensure that the children can wander at will and return to tents or not as the case may be. The children will also move the resources from tent to tent, along the pathways, and this opens up more possibilities to explore within each tent.

Stage two – explore the theme

1 Big tent: Inside the big tent provide opportunities to mark-make on the paper that is taped to the floor, ensuring there is a wide range of tools available. Comment on the patterns the children are making, point out any similarities to the pathways and encourage the children to extend their line of thought by introducing items such as small world play equipment, people, cars, animals. For some children, just being inside the tent will be an experience to respond to and may stimulate a discussion about camping experiences.

2 First pop-up tent: Inside this tent install a toy puppet in a bed. Explain to the children that s/he is feeling shy because s/he has no friends and suggest that they might make a friend out of the available materials in the tent. These could be a selection of cardboard tubes, paper, wool and tape – anything to make a puppet friend. We found that the children loved working in an enclosed space and stayed focused on the task, for example the little girl in Figure 2.1 made a puppet which travelled round with her for the rest of the session. Engage the children in conversation about their puppet as they personalise it and encourage language to describe the materials they have used and textures they can feel. Some children might leave their finished puppet in the tent and some might take it on the journey with them.

3 Second pop-up tent: Inside this tent provide a variety of sensory experiences for the children to explore. For example, hang mobiles and shiny materials from the roof of the tent and arrange a selection of textured materials on the floor of the tent. You could also provide plastic mirrors and a few instruments. Encourage the children to try out different positions, maybe seeing what the roof of the tent looks like if they lie down.

4 Third pop-up tent: This tent is decorated in a jungle theme, with netting over the top of it and inside is a variety of toy wild animals of all sizes. You could include artificial flowers, big leaves and perhaps a pond made out of shiny foil for

Figure 2.1   A few carefully selected resources will make a 'friend' for the puppet inside the tent

the animals to drink from. A tape playing appropriate music would add to the atmosphere. Also in the tent have available some colour swatches which the children can use to identify colours and to match the colours to the animals.

5 Fourth pop-up tent: In this tent supply a favourite story book with relevant props. It would link well to choose a story that includes the concept of a journey, which the children could discuss and maybe role play. We chose *Harry, the Dirty Dog* by Gene Zion and Margaret Bloy Graham, and we provided a baby bath with water, a scrubbing brush, flannel, sponge and bubbles and of course a scruffy-looking toy dog. The children will be able to observe the different effects of water on materials and consider the best way to wash a dog to get it really clean. Some of our children were keen to explore the possibilities of a 'dog washing machine'. Paper and mark-making tools can be available for the children to record their experience.

Stage three – ideas to extend the theme
1. Invite the children to make their own tent using the bendy tent poles which can be taped together with pieces of pre-cut gaffer tape. Encourage them to decorate their tent with strips of material, or wool, or to make their own decorations. Take photos as they make them because you will probably not be able to keep them for long.

2. Give the children small rolls of paper and invite them to roll them out on the floor to make new pathways, and watch what else they use them for. Our group

Figure 2.2   This little boy took his own direction of learning by bandaging up his leg with the till roll tape

started to lay more 'track' for the trains to run on and one little boy began to use them as bandages, developing a doctor's role-play situation, as illustrated by Figure 2.2 He initially began exploring the potential of wrapping the tape around his leg as he had seen his mother do to him when he had hurt himself, and quickly gathered other interested children around him. A mini impromptu role-play situation developed which the practitioners were able to develop at a further stage.

Stage four – recall the theme

When you feel the children have had enough time to explore the possibilities, gather them together in the big tent. Using the drawing on the floor as a starting point, encourage the children to talk about their different exploration experiences with the assortment of materials and the pathways they took.

Assessment opportunities

Practitioners would be able to identify learning styles for future planning and observe developmental skills. The level of the children's cooperative play would be evident. A group book including photographs and children's quotes about the experience would be a valuable addition to the setting.

Ways forward

Practitioners might want to follow up the children's interests and further explore the possibilities of materials. For example, try designing and making a dog washing machine.

■ Take a story as a starting point to explore the possibilities of developing movement and dance ideas with the children.

Example 2B   Movement and dance activity

ACTIVITY PLAN

Theme:
▸ Going on a bear hunt.

Creative arts activity:
▸ Exploring dramatic movement.

Why?
▸ Group theme, which has already been explored through visual art.

Suggested resources:
▸ We're Going on a Bear Hunt, retold by Michael Rosen (Walker Books, 2001).
▸ An assortment of materials to support the actions, for example brown fabric or non-slip mats.
▸ Sticks with white ribbons or crepe paper stuck on them.
▸ Parachute.
▸ Musical instruments – rainmakers, claves, tambourines.
▸ CD player with appropriate music.
▸ A big parachute suspended to make the bear's cave. This needs to be set up before the activity begins.
▸ Hoops.

Suggested questions to ask:
▸ Where would you look for a bear?
▸ How would you feel on the journey?
▸ Why are you hunting a bear?

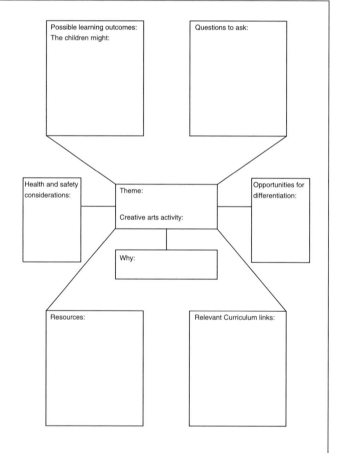

Possible learning outcomes: The children might:

Questions to ask:

Health and safety considerations:

Theme:

Creative arts activity:

Opportunities for differentiation:

Why:

Resources:

Relevant Curriculum links:

Possible learning outcomes:
The children might:
▶ *Enjoy joining in with dancing games.*
▶ *Imitate and create movement in response to music.*
▶ *Begin to move rhythmically. Develop a repertoire of actions by putting a sequence of movements together.*

Opportunities for differentiation:
▶ *Size of group – can be adjusted to enable adults to really observe and support the children.*

Relevant curriculum links:
▶ *CLL – recording the journey; writing to the bear.*
▶ *KUW – features of objects and living things; sense of place.*

Health and safety considerations:
▶ *Floor surface.*
▶ *Sticks for ribbons.*

Exploration process

Stage one – introduce the theme

1. Read the story to the children and discuss the concept of the hunt. Why are they going and how do the children think they are feeling?

2. Make up a tune to the chorus of the story. Anything will do as long as it's simple. Sing it a few times to establish it firmly in the children's minds.

3. Explain to the children that they are going to explore the idea of going to find a bear. First they are going to think about the different ways they might have to move.

4. Taking suggestions from the children, using available space, explore movements such as creeping on tiptoe, marching bravely, crawling on hands and knees. Make sure you comment on unusual actions as well as those of children who have observed and copied yours.

5. Tell the children that they are going to begin the search for the bear and may come across some of the situations in the story. If you attempt to interpret the whole story it can become laboured and young children tend to lose concentration so it is better to choose perhaps three ideas for movement and change them round another time.

Stage two – develop the theme

1. Invite the children to sing the 'bear hunt song' as they begin their journey. They could be holding hands with a friend or following in a line. Take the suggestions from them.

2. The first situation you could explore is the thick oozy mud, which we represented by the brown material and non-slip mats. The children will need to stop to see if they can go over, under or through it but will probably realise that they will need to put on their boots.

3. Together explore movements, which suggest the squelch of the words in the book. These could be very slow exaggerated actions in which the children lift their knees up high and place their feet down very carefully to avoid getting completely stuck in the mud. Encourage the children to make good use of all the space. You could select a piece of music to interpret this action or use instruments, such as the rainmakers and drums.

4. Recall the story and lead the children into another adventure, such as the big dark forest, and whisper about how you all feel about going into it. Discuss with the children which movements would illustrate the 'stumble trip' words in the book and devise a short sequence. For example, stamp, stamp and then lunge forward onto hands keeping feet on the floor. Encourage the children to keep the movements slow to start off with and keep the rhythm by saying the words all together. Again you could then support this movement with music or instruments, such as claves or wood blocks.

5. Once through the wood continue on the journey, moving in a chosen manner, until maybe you are surrounded by the swirling, whirling snowstorm. Using the ribbons on sticks or even just hand-held strips of white crepe paper, explore whirling round movements at all levels. Again, keep the pace slow initially and introduce music or instruments if required. Don't forget the voice is an instrument and can be used very effectively.

6. Invite the children to gather together as the snowstorm finishes and they sink down to the ground, to have a rest. The 'bear cave' or in our case, the big parachute, is now in sight.

Stage three – conclude the theme

1. Recall the ending of the story and initiate a discussion about the bear, whether it is scary or, as our children decided, is it really lonely and needing a friend to play with? The illustration on the last page of the book would support this theory. Finish the story in a way that is meaningful to the children. This is the ending that our children decided on.

Figure 2.3   The use of hoops controlled the dance activity as well as giving children the opportunity to work co-operatively

2. Sing the bear hunt song as you march into the cave because you are going to ask the bear to be friends and join in the dance. Using the coloured hoops either individually or with a partner move to some music or the song. Encourage the children to explore ways in which they can move in a controlled manner if they are using circular movements, as illustrated in Figure 2.3. These children really responded to the use of hoops and negotiating movements with a partner.

3. Finish the activity in the bear's cave, perhaps by lying down quietly singing the bear hunt song.

Assessment opportunities

Practitioners would be able to observe the children's ability to recall the story and the imaginative way in which they created movements.

Ways forward

Children could put together a short sequence of the movements they had explored. They could also demonstrate a movement and their peers would have to guess which part of the journey they were describing.

Practitioners might want to explore further the use of instruments to interpret the story.

Example 2C   Music activity

ACTIVITY PLAN

Theme:
▸ Going on a bear hunt

Creativity arts activity:
▸ Exploring qualities of instruments, including the voice

Why?
▸ Links to a previous exploration of movement and dance.

Suggested resources:
▸ We're Going on a Bear Hunt, retold by Michael Rosen (Walker Books, 2001).
▸ Range of musical instruments to produce different sounds.
▸ Range of beaters to use with them, some covered in material.

Suggested questions to ask:
▸ What kind of a sound would a big bear make?
▸ Can your voice make a sound like that instrument?

Possible learning outcomes:
The children might:
▸ Show an interest in the way musical instruments sound.
▸ Tap out simple repeated rhythms and make some up.
▸ Explore and learn how sounds can be changed.
▸ Explore the different sounds of instruments.

Opportunities for differentiation:
▸ A variety of instruments to suit a range of developmental abilities.

Relevant curriculum links:
▸ KUW – designing and making and recording sounds

Health and safety considerations:
▸ Appropriate use of instruments.

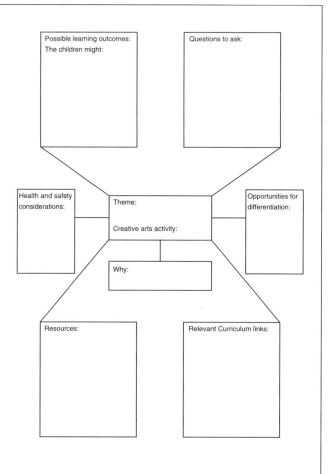

Exploration process

You will have previously read the story.

Stage one – introduce the theme

1. Display a wide range of instruments for the children to look at. These will include:

- Instruments to tap/beat, such as wood blocks, tambours, triangles.
- Instruments to shake, such as tambourines, egg shakers, maracas.
- Instruments to pluck, such as a guitar.
- You will also need materials such as plastic bubble wrap, silver foil.

2. Invite the children to play with the instruments and see what kinds of sounds they can produce. Involve yourself in the exploration of sound and comment on the sounds that you are hearing. Encourage the children to make comparisons, for example 'it sounds like a lot of leaves shaking'. At this stage these comparisons do not have to relate to the story. Make sure that children use this opportunity to experiment with the whole range of instruments and encourage any ideas of using the instruments in a different way, as illustrated by Figure 2.4, such as scratching the surface of the tambourines or using a beater with material on it to soften the sound.

Figure 2.4   These children are experimenting with sounds to recreate a 'big bear' sound

Stage two – develop the theme

1. Recall with the children the experiences in the story and suggest that they might try to identify instruments to imitate the descriptive words in the story. At this stage remind the children about their voices, which are also instruments. The more opportunities the children have to experiment with instruments the easier and more imaginatively they will tackle this task. These are some ideas that our children produced:

- Swishy swashy – bubble wrap, rainmakers, egg shakers, maracas.

- Splash splosh – beaters on plastic bubble wrap.

- Squelch squerch – Scraping a beater on a raised wooden surface.

- Stumble trip – woodblocks, tambour or drums, as illustrated by Figure 4 on the companion website.

- Hoooo woooo – voices, shouting into hollow containers.

You could also experiment with the kind of sounds that the bear would make. For example, if it were a big bear how would it growl? What about a very little bear? Encourage the children to use their voices to 'growl' into tambours or containers in a loud and quiet way.

Section three – recall the theme

1. Remind the children about the sequence of the story and discuss which instruments they should use to imitate the descriptive words in the story.

2. Using a white board or piece of paper make a sound story board, drawing simple symbols of the chosen instruments in their correct sequence to match the story.

3. Invite children to play the instruments in sequence with the rest of the group saying the words.

Assessment opportunities

Practitioners would be able to observe individual children's listening and imaginative skills. The sound story sequences could be recorded visually and using a tape recorder.

Ways forward

Further sessions could explore designing and making opportunities to create new instruments to describe sounds or emotions.

Example activities starting from the visual arts (2)

Example 2D   Visual art activity

ACTIVITY PLAN

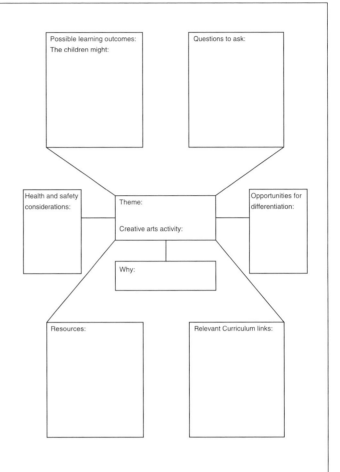

Theme:
▶ Insects.

Creative arts activity:
▶ Using materials to create and decorate.

Why?
▶ Theme within setting.

Suggested resources:
▶ Rolls of one-sided, wide sticky tape.
▶ Shoe boxes containing items such as small toy insects, sequins, buttons, natural objects, foil cut into strips.
▶ Plastic mirrors.

Suggested questions to ask:
▶ How do you feel in here?
▶ How would your insect move?

Possible learning outcomes:
The children might:
▶ Make comparisons and create new connections.
▶ Create three-dimensional structures.

Opportunities for differentiation:
▶ Adult/peer support for children who feel uncertain in an enclosed space.

Relevant curriculum links:
▶ KUW – living things, materials.
▶ MD – pattern.

Health and safety considerations:
▶ Number of children in a small space.

Exploration process

You will need to have set up the following scene either in a small room, a corner of a room or an outside shed.

Using one-sided, wide sticky tape, stretch lengths of it across the area to make a spider's web effect, using all levels.

Put some interesting items that the children will be able to stick on to the tape in several shoe boxes, for example a selection of small toy insects, some strips of foil or coloured plastic, large sequins or buttons, natural objects like pieces of grass, leaves. Wrap up the boxes in coloured paper and leave by the web.

Stage one – introduce the theme

1. Encourage the children to sit in a circle and show them a large toy spider explaining that this will give them a clue about what they are going to be thinking about.

2. Sing 'Incy, Wincy, Spider' all together and discuss the idea of a spider's web and what it is used for.

    ■ Invite the children to come and visit the spider's web that you have created.

Stage two – develop the theme

1. Carefully enter the area with the web – the children will quickly realise that the web is sticky but that nothing is caught on it. Allow them time to adjust to the space and settle down. Some children may be unsure of this situation so make sure there is someone to support them, sitting outside the web if necessary.

2. 'Find' the boxes and, taking one box at a time, choose a child to shake it, trying to guess what might be inside. Once the child has opened the box, discuss the items all together and suggest that these things could be used to decorate the spider's web.

3. Demonstrate, if necessary, to the children how the items will just stick onto the sticky tape web and hang there. Encourage all the children to have a go, as illustrated by Figure 2.5. We noticed how some children arranged items very carefully, almost making a sequence, while others were completely random in their sticking. Once all the boxes have been opened and used discuss the look of the web with the children. Do they think the spider will like it? Could they make some more things to hang on it?

Stage three – extend the theme

Have three tables ready for different activities, of which the children can attend all or one, or stay playing in the web:

■ Table One contains materials to stimulate the children to make their own insects, for example card tubes, coloured plastics, pipecleaners, ribbon, glue, tape. Practitioners should support the children by encouraging them to talk about their insect and the qualities of the materials being used.

Figure 2.5   The installation of a spider's web allows for a wide range of creative and sensory opportunities

- Table Two contains card cut into small hoops with an assortment of materials that the children can use to make 'dream catchers'. They could use sticky tape to reproduce the web theme on the hoop and decorate it with feathers and sequins etc. The dream catchers need to be attached to wool so they can be hung on to the spider's web as they are completed.

- Table Three contains an assortment of shiny materials, glitter, sequins, silver paint and thin card. Tell the children they are going to make some stars, discussing the shapes they might need. Some children will readily cut their own star shapes and some might need support but you should end up with different size and shape stars rather than lots of pre-cut stars all looking exactly the same. Encourage the children to decorate their star and attach some wool to hang it.

Stage four – recall the theme

1. Invite the children back into the spider's web and discuss the insects that some of the children will have made. Encourage the children to think about how their insect might move and talk about the process of making it and the types of materials they used.

2. Tell the children that it is almost night time and time for the insects to go to sleep. Darken the room if possible, discussing what might happen in the sky at

night time and hang up the stars on the spider's web. If you have access to fairy lights they would make a lovely addition to the night time scene.

3. Invite the children to lie down in the spider's web and look at the lights and shiny stars. You could play some appropriate music to close the session.

Assessment opportunities

The practitioners would be able to make observations of developmental skills in using tools and materials. An illustrated book of the children's feelings about the experience would offer children the opportunity to recall the activity and share it with their families.

Ways forward

In our sessions the children were very interested in the star theme and this could be taken further.

The children's ideas about how their insects moved might be explored through some movement and dance activities.

Example 2E   Movement and dance activity

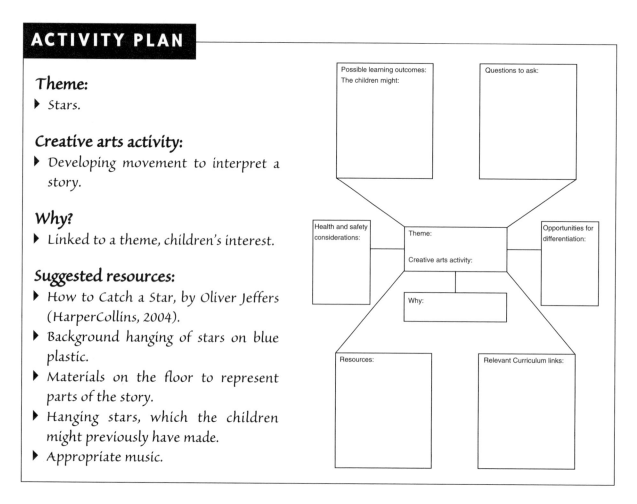

ACTIVITY PLAN

Theme:
▶ Stars.

Creative arts activity:
▶ Developing movement to interpret a story.

Why?
▶ Linked to a theme, children's interest.

Suggested resources:
▶ How to Catch a Star, by Oliver Jeffers (HarperCollins, 2004).
▶ Background hanging of stars on blue plastic.
▶ Materials on the floor to represent parts of the story.
▶ Hanging stars, which the children might previously have made.
▶ Appropriate music.

Possible learning outcomes: The children might:

Questions to ask:

Health and safety considerations:

Theme:

Creative arts activity:

Opportunities for differentiation:

Why:

Resources:

Relevant Curriculum links:

Suggested questions to ask:

▶ Do you have a special friend?
▶ What kind of things do you do together?
▶ What sort of sounds could you make to sound like a star?
▶ Can you make a pattern?

Possible learning outcomes:

The children might:

▶ Develop a repertoire of actions by putting a sequence of movements together.
▶ Play cooperatively as part of a group to act out a narrative.
▶ Imitate and create movement in response to music.

Opportunities for differentiation:

▶ Space.
▶ Adult support.

Relevant curriculum links:

▶ CLL – Own stories about friendship.
▶ KUW – World around us.

Health and safety considerations:

▶ Floor surface.

Exploration process

Stage one – introduce the theme

1. Gather the children in the space which has been decorated with materials and stars to support the story. We incorporated a climbing frame into the space to include the possibilities of working at different levels.

2. Read the story to the children, pointing out the materials that are around them, for example some material to represent the sand and sea. When the story is finished recall the basic theme and suggest that they could make up a dance about the story.

Stage two – develop the theme

1. Introduce the idea of reaching for a star, developing stretching movements and encouraging the children to use all levels. For example, they could start from a sitting position and stretch out their arms in different directions and then try the same actions but from a standing position. At all times the practitioners should be modelling the movements and commenting on individual children's efforts.

2. Give half the group a card star and invite them to develop a slow, long, lunge-type movement in which they pass their star to another child and so on, creating

Figure 2.6   The children are developing stretching movements from a variety of positions

a continuum of movement, as is illustrated by Figure 2.6. This could be supported by some appropriate music.

3. Continuing the slow theme, invite the children to pretend to be walking in space, developing the movement of lifting their knees and placing their feet down carefully and slowly. How would they move their arms and heads?

4. Invite the children to slowly sink down and 'land' on the moon, which is the round silver piece of material. Describe the actions that they have just been doing and ensure that you praise their participation in the dance.

Stage three – develop a sequence
1. With the children sitting on the moon, discuss the idea of a shooting star and just practise shooting an arm out in different directions, on command. You could use an instrument such as a short shake on a tambourine to give the command.

2. Standing up in a space, encourage the children to suggest a word or sounds to describe a shooting star and then an action to accompany the word. Once the children have all practised these they can be put together into a simple sequence. This is the sequence our children made up.

■ Shoot – jump up stretching two arms above the head.

■ Wizz – lunge out an arm.

■ Star jump – make a star jump with both arms and legs outstretched.

■ ZZZZZ – whirl to the ground like a falling star.

3. If the children are developmentally ready for this you could then develop the theme from the story of the little boy finding a friend. We gave each child a partner and encouraged one child to make a movement which the other child had to copy and then to swap over. Some children used the sequence we had just developed and some children investigated new ideas. This is a difficult concept for young children so comment on actions and praise all efforts.

4. To end the session invite all the group to lie down quietly on the moon to listen to some calm music, thinking about the story and their dance.

Assessment opportunities

Either a book with annotated photographs recording the dance or a video recording would provide an opportunity for practitioners to evaluate a child's level of participation and ability to recall and respond to the activity.

Ways forward

The idea of working with a partner could be further explored.

Example 2F   Music activity

ACTIVITY PLAN

Theme:
▶ Stars

Creative arts activity:
▶ Identification of musical sounds and beginnings of composition.

Why?
▶ Previous exploration of dance and partner work.

Suggested questions to ask:
▶ Turn-taking questions.

Suggested resources:

▸ *How to Catch a Star*, by Oliver Jeffers (HarperCollins, 2004).

▸ If possible, create a sparkly space with hanging stars, silver tinsel. You could also hang instruments like Indian bells from the tinsel.

▸ Range of instruments, including xylophones, triangles, Indian bells, sleigh bells.

▸ Ensure you have two of each kind of instrument.

Possible learning outcomes:

The children might:

▸ Show an interest in the way musical instruments sound.

▸ Sing a few simple, familiar songs.

▸ Tap out simple repeated rhythms and make some up.

▸ Explore the different sounds of instruments.

Opportunities for differentiation:

▸ Size of group.

▸ Adult support.

Relevant curriculum links:

▸ KUW – Designing and making.

Health and safety considerations:

▸ Appropriate use of instruments.

Possible learning outcomes: The children might:	Questions to ask:

Health and safety considerations:	Theme: Creative arts activity:	Opportunities for differentiation:

Why:

Resources:	Relevant Curriculum links:

Exploration process

Stage one – introduce the theme

1. Invite the children to gather in the sparkly space and allow them time to discuss what they can see. Either read the story or remind them about it and ask them to suggest a song they know well about a star.

2. Sing 'Twinkle, twinkle, little star', all together.

3. Introduce the xylophones, triangles, Indian bells and sleigh bells and invite each child to choose one to play. Sing the song again accompanied by the instruments, as shown in Figure 2.7, encouraging the children to keep a steady beat, and then change the instruments around once to allow children the opportunity to play something different.

Figure 2.7   A stimulating environment will encourage children to feel involved in the task of accompanying a song

4. Experiment by playing loudly or quietly, fast or slow, and ask the children which version they prefer. You could record the versions to listen to another time.

Stage two – develop the theme

1. Tell the children that they are going to be listening carefully to the sounds the instruments make and see if they can match the sounds.

2. Set up a divider – this could be a piece of starry material, suspended between two chairs. Arrange one set of identical instruments (no more than four to start off with) on either side of the divider. Initially choose instruments that sound very different, like a drum, a triangle, a maracca and bells.

3. Choose a child to sit on each side of the divider (no peeping) and ask one child to choose an instrument to play. When the other child thinks he or she has identified the instrument they can play the one they think it is. Involve the rest of the group by asking them to nod their heads if they think it is the same or shake their heads if they disagree.

4. As the children gain in confidence, make the game more challenging by using instruments that sound similar, for example, a maraca and an egg shaker, a clave and a woodblock.

Stage three – extend the theme

1. For those children who are developmentally ready, introduce the idea of working with a partner, copying a pattern. Adult support is initially really important for this process until the children grasp the concept of the exercise, which requires quite complex cooperative skills, as shown in Figure 5 on the companion website.

2. Invite each child to work with a friend, each using the same type of instrument. Encourage one child to develop a short musical phrase, for example three taps on a tambourine followed by a long shake followed by three more taps. The second child then needs to copy the pattern. The developmental ability of the children will dictate the level to which this activity can be taken.

3. Some children will be able to scribe their musical pattern to read and play using their own form of notation.

4. Invite the children to share their patterns with the group.

Assessment opportunities

Practitioners can record the children's playing and musical patterns and take photographs to support an interactive display to encourage children to try to copy the musical patterns.

The child's developing listening skills can be observed, while any particular interests can be identified and encouraged, as shown in Figure 6 on the companion website.

Ways forward

Ensure that instruments are available in the learning environment for children to explore and develop their composition skills.

CHAPTER 3

Starting from music

This chapter will give you ideas of ways to develop musical activities by:

- Highlighting the importance of music in the early years.
- Offering practical solutions to common concerns.
- Illustrating two musical activities each leading into an exploration of visual art and dance.

Music is not just about singing songs and playing instruments. Children can be challenged to recognise different sounds and to explore how they can be changed, either for fun or to accompany another activity. They can begin to identify repeated sounds and sound patterns and they will love matching movements to music. Even young children are able to respond to the concepts of pitch, rhythm and tempo.

Music plays an important role in developing creative awareness in young children in the following ways.

- It allows for an alternative form of communication and an opportunity to express emotions.

- It is a fun activity which can provide opportunities to perform.

- It can encourage the development of cooperative skills.

- It can stimulate problem solving explorations.

- It encourages children to explore the quality of sound and the way sounds can be put together.

- It emerges very naturally in children's play and connects easily to other art forms, thus enriching the activity.

Many practitioners feel apprehensive about planning for and delivering music sessions. The following advice may help you feel more confident.

! DON'T PANIC IF...

I can't sing or keep in tune.
It won't stop the children enjoying the activity and you can choose songs they are familiar with so they can help you. There are also loads of rhymes and raps you can use as an alternative to singing as well as CDs to sing along with. However, it is best not to rely on these all the time because you cannot get a true indication of the quality of the children's participation.

I feel embarrassed singing in front of other adults.
Tell them how you feel. Maybe you can all sing together to begin with. Singing does not have to be a whole group experience, so what about starting off with a few children in a quiet corner?

I don't know many songs.
There are lots of great books you can buy or borrow (see Further reading). You can also make up songs with the children using any well-known tune, like 'London Bridge is falling down' or 'Row, row, row your boat'.

I can't play the piano/any instrument.
It doesn't matter. Have fun exploring the percussion instruments with the children.

I'm worried it will get chaotic when I bring out the instruments.
It won't if you plan it carefully and perhaps introduce a few of the same type at a time. For example instruments you play by shaking. You will have some ground rules about taking care of the instruments and storing them properly, so the children will understand that they are a valuable resource.

We don't have enough money for many instruments.
Buy a few good quality ones and make the rest with the children.

The following two sections demonstrate ways in which music activities could lead into an exploration of other creative art forms.

Examples of activities starting from music (1)

Example 3A   Music activity

ACTIVITY PLAN

Theme:
▶ *Going on a musical journey.*

Creative arts activity:
▶ *Exploration of sound.*

Why?

▶ A good abstract theme.

Suggested resources:

▶ Materials to make a den-these could be drapes tied across a small room, or with a small group you could use a pop-up tent.
▶ A selection of instruments in the den.
▶ Outside space.

Suggested questions to ask:

▶ What will we need to go on a journey?
▶ What sounds can we hear?
▶ How can we make sounds?

Possible learning outcomes – the children might:

▶ Tap out simple repeated rhythms.
▶ Explore how sounds can be changed.
▶ Explore the different sounds of instruments.
▶ Respond to sound with body movement.

Opportunities for differentiation:

▶ A range of instruments that allows for large and small motor control skills.
▶ Adult support – some children feel uneasy in small enclosed spaces.

Relevant curriculum links:

▶ CLL – stories like Peace at last, by Jill Murphy (Macmillan, 1995).
▶ KUW – designing own instruments to make sounds they have discovered.

Health and safety considerations:

▶ Number of children in small space.

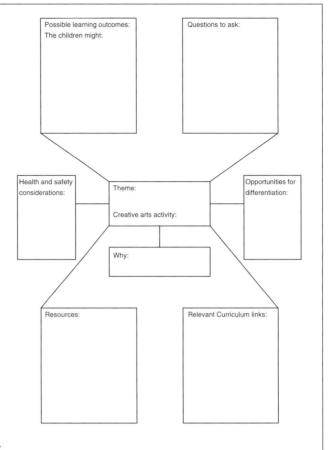

Exploration process

Stage one – introduce the theme

1. Ensure the children are sitting in a circle. Play a name clapping game to focus their attention.

2. Tell the children that they are going to go to a special den to find some instruments to play, one of which will be a magic instrument which will take them on a journey. The children will not need to take anything apart from their bodies as they will be exploring their senses. The following dialogue incorporates identification of body parts with a variety of sounds. The adult models the response with the children:

'Have you got your **big** voices?' 'Yes we have.'
'Have you got your **low** voices?' 'Yes we have.'
'Have you got your **quiet** hands?' 'Yes we have.'
'Have you got your **lou**d feet?' 'Yes we have.'

The children will make many more suggestions and you can choose one action, for example hopping, to lead the children into the den.

Stage two – develop the theme

1. Inside the den encourage the children to explore the different instruments and comment on the types of sounds they are making. An empty bottle from a water cooler, as illustrated by Figure 7 on the companion website, proved to be a popular choice and a good example of introducing children to alternative types of instruments.

2. Remind the children that they are looking for a magic instrument to take them on their journey. Invite each child to play an instrument in turn and discuss the sound together. Is it high or low, loud or quiet? What kind of quality do we want in this magic instrument?

3. Together decide which instrument it will be, then the child who is playing that instrument will be the leader to take you out on the journey.

4. As you go outside discuss the ways in which you could move to the sound of the magic instrument. Perhaps the children could form a long line and tiptoe, varying levels, or if it is a loud sound you could march outside, keeping the beat.

Stage three – explore the theme

Once outside, explain to the children that they are going to discover how many different sounds they can hear outside. They will need to listen carefully and look for things that might make a sound. (You will have previously ensured that there are no dangerous items in the outside space that the children might pick up.)

- Listening: encourage the children to lie down and shut their eyes. Give them time to really listen before you question them. We were told, 'I can hear a bumble bee', and 'I can hear the birds'. This was a rural space and in your space the children might hear horns, buses and aeroplanes, which is fine because the children are still demonstrating good listening skills. Remember the sounds they have identified because you are going to use them later.

- Finding: encourage the children to search and pick up stones, wood, grass, plastic. What do they have to do to find out if it will make a sound?

Figure 3.1   The children are listening carefully to find out if their found objects will make a sound

One example of what our children explored is shown in Figure 3.1. We noticed a child stroking the wall with a feather to listen to the sound and then some children discovered the big tyres and started beating them with their hands: 'Wow, we're making a pattern'. When we provided them with beaters they discovered that the sound changed. The little boy in Figure 3.2 was unperturbed by not having a tyre to beat – he simply found an alternative. One child picked a small piece of bush and brushed it on the ground. Some children found a spider inside a tyre: 'He's very quiet. Can we sing 'Incy Wincy Spider' very quietly so we don't scare him?'

When you feel the possibilities have been explored, ask a child to play the magic instrument to gather the group together and return to the den.

Stage four – recalling the theme

1. Discuss with the children the sounds you all heard and made, repeating the vocabulary that you heard the children use.

2. Draw the children's attention to the instruments in the den and ask the question, 'Will any of these instruments make a sound like the bumble bees?' Use the other examples and find out what the children think.

Figure 3.2   An upturned bucket will make as good a sound as a drum

3. Ask the children, 'Can we still hear those sounds now?' 'Why not?' We were told, 'No, because we're inside and we can hear the babies upstairs crying!'

4. Choose a short piece of music to listen to as a way of finishing the session.

Assessment opportunities

Practitioners would be able to identify children who were able to stay focused on the task and make observations on the children's preferred learning styles. In our sessions practitioners were able to observe that some children who showed little response in a group situation really blossomed in the outdoor exploration, coming up with some very creative ideas.

Photographs would clearly illustrate the involvement of the children and a group book about the journey incorporating photographs and the children's comments would provide a good recall opportunity for the children and a means of sharing the experience with families.

Ways forward

In our sessions practitioners identified a need to build more planned music sessions into the schedule and to take the instruments outside more often.

Some of the children might be able to develop the idea of composition using instruments to describe the journey they made.

The theme of bumble bees and insects was established very firmly by the children and in our sessions and offers an idea that could easily be explored further.

Example 3B   Visual art activity

ACTIVITY PLAN

Theme:
▶ Insects.

Creative arts activity:
▶ Exploration of light and shadow.

Why?
▶ Follow-up on interest previously established by children through a music session.

Suggested resources:
▶ Outside space – but it could work inside.
▶ One big light box – a hinged wooden box with the lid made of white sheeting will work well.
▶ A selection of small light boxes, for example a shoe box with 6×6 cm holes cut out of the top and one end. We covered the boxes in shiny paper to make them more stimulating.
▶ Decorative items, shiny balls, anything that will make an interesting shadow.
▶ A big piece of white sheeting.
▶ Small torches.
▶ Pieces of coloured gel/acetate/cellophane.
▶ Scissors.
▶ Sticky-backed plastic.

Possible learning outcomes: The children might:

Questions to ask:

Health and safety considerations:

Theme:

Creative arts activity:

Opportunities for differentiation:

Why:

Resources:

Relevant Curriculum links:

▶ Pieces of plain white paper.
▶ A selection of toy insects and animals, all different sizes.
▶ Black card cut into picture frame shape.

Suggested questions to ask:
▶ What does it look like?
▶ Where does the shadow come from?
▶ Can we do this inside?

Possible learning outcomes:
The children might:
▶ Explore and experience using a range of senses and movements.
▶ Explore colour and differentiate between colours.
▶ Use their bodies to explore space.
▶ Combine media to create new effects.
▶ Use ideas involving fitting, overlapping.

Opportunities for differentiation:
▶ Size of the group – ensure you have enough equipment for everyone.
▶ Adult support.

Relevant curriculum links:
▶ CLL – stories that would develop the insect theme, for example The Very Hungry Caterpillar and The Bad Tempered Ladybird, both by Eric Carle.
▶ KUW – further investigation into light properties, using kaleidoscopes and light prisms.
▶ MD – vocabulary, tessellation with shapes.

Health and safety considerations:
▶ Possible glare on white sheeting.

Exploration process

Stage one – introduce the theme

1. Hide the empty small light boxes around the outside space. Tell the children that they need to go and see if they can find some shiny boxes and watch and see what they do with them. In our setting the younger children were happy to build up a collection in the box that they could shake and in some cases hold onto for the entire session, while the older children began to sort their findings and realised that the hole in the side enabled them to view the item.

2. Encourage the children to show each other their discoveries. Discuss how they can see the object in the box. Why isn't it too dark to see it?

Figure 3.3   Investigating light and shadow with a simple light box

3. Introduce the small torches to them as another means of creating light. One of our children demonstrated an interesting use of vocabulary as he proudly declared, 'Look, I've torched the lion.'

Stage two – develop the theme
1. Introduce the group to the big light box. Hold up an object behind the white sheet lid ensuring that the children are in front to see the shadow. Ask them questions such as:

- What does it look like?
- How does it work?
- Where does the shadow come from?
- What will happen if we shine the torch?

As shown by Figure 3.3, the children will be keen to try it out for themselves. At this stage it would be useful to have another adult to support the activity, to ensure that some children watch while one or two children make the shadows. Our children had a choice of items to make shadows with but very quickly discovered the insects, particularly the big hairy spider.

2. Provide the children with a sheet of white paper and let them discover how all objects have a shadow if there is enough light. Some of our children began tracing round the shadow with their fingers.

Stage three – introduce some colour

1. Provide the children with some pieces of coloured gel/acetate and watch what they do with it. One little girl disappeared with a piece of pink gel and then proudly produced her light box saying, 'My slug has gone pink!' as she held the gel over the hole on the top of the box which currently contained a small slug called Stephanie! The children will realise that they can use the gel on the big light box to create coloured shadows.

2. Provide the children with squares of black card cut into a picture frame shape with sticky backed plastic stuck to one side. The children can then easily stick random shapes of coloured gel or sweet wrappers to the sticky side of the plastic, experimenting with overlapping and colour investigation. We found this activity captivated the girls instantly but needed more adult support to absorb the boys.

3. The boys were in fact fully absorbed in a project of their own. One child chose to hang a shiny ball on a nearby bush and came running to tell me about his 'Christmas tree', insisting we took a picture of it, as illustrated by Figure 3.4. Very soon his friends were joining in and the bush became beautifully decorated.

Figure 3.4   This boy is absorbed in decorating a bush using resources which were put out with a different purpose in mind

Stage four – go bigger

1. Suspend the big piece of white sheeting and encourage the children to use their whole body to make big shadows as well as continuing to use the objects from the light box collection. We found that an ugly bug ball soon emerged, with larger than life insects.

Assessment opportunities

Practitioners could make a wide range of developmental observations on the children, supported by photographs of their participation.

We found that the process of introducing items at different stages worked well, as the children were not swamped with too many possibilities at once.

Ways forward

The practitioners in our settings found that the children really identified with the light boxes.

- ■ Future activities could explore other ideas with these.

- ■ The idea of decoration, which arose spontaneously during our sessions, offered other activities to pursue.

Example 3C   Movement and dance activity

ACTIVITY PLAN

Theme:
▶ Going on a journey.

Creative arts activity:
▶ Taking a journey with the children, finding items on the way to develop a variety of movements culminating in a sequential pattern.

Why?
▶ To explore further the idea of going on a journey and to develop a different art form, which might include the idea of decoration.

Suggested resources:
▶ Indoor and outdoor space if possible, but this activity could all take place inside.
▶ One small child-size empty suitcase.
▶ Three shoe boxes covered in shiny paper with one set of objects in each box as follows:

Possible learning outcomes:
The children might:

Questions to ask:

Health and safety considerations:

Theme:

Creative arts activity:

Opportunities for differentiation:

Why:

Resources:

Relevant Curriculum links:

1　A selection of toy sea animals.

2　A selection of toy hippos and elephants.

3　A selection of toy butterflies.

▶ Coloured ribbons on short sticks, enough for at least one per child.

▶ A big piece of blue cloth with a selection of plastic fish.

▶ A suitcase full of beautiful materials and special dressing up clothes/artificial flowers, beads, hats etc.

▶ Small, round, non-slip mats (for example bath mats) – one for each child taking part in the activity.

▶ Message written in box and coloured card spot to match small round mats.

Suggested questions to ask:

▶ Where do you think we will go?

▶ What might we find on the way?

▶ How do you feel?

▶ What do you think might go in this empty suitcase?

Possible learning outcomes:

The children might:

▶ Make sense of what they see, hear, smell, touch and feel.

▶ Capture experiences and responses with movement and dance.

▶ Develop a sequence of movements.

Opportunities for differentiation:

▶ Size of group.

▶ Adult support.

Relevant curriculum links:

▶ CLL – writing messages with instructions for a journey.

▶ KUW – living things.

Health and safety considerations:

▶ Appropriate use of equipment.

Exploration process

Stage one – introduce the theme

1. You will previously have set up the outside area by 'hiding' the shoe boxes in appropriate places. Distribute the small mats to resemble stepping stones, which the children will use to start their journey.

2. Gather the children in a group and show them a small shoe box. Choose a child to open it and look inside. There is a message saying 'We are going on a journey and to find the way you have to search for the spots that look like this'. Also inside the box is a card spot the same colour as the small round mats.

3. Produce the empty suitcase. What could it be for? Tell the children that they will take it on the journey and see what they can find.

4. Begin the journey by looking for the small mats. Encourage everyone to stand on one.

Stage two – explore the theme

1. Ask the children 'What do these spots look like?' Our children said 'puddles', so we decided to do some warming up exercises before we set off on the journey. We put on our wellington boots and then:

- Stamped up and down in our own puddle.

- Shook our hands, shook our feet.

- Jumped on the spot with two feet together.

You could take any suggestion and develop some movements to get the children moving together. The length of time the next part of this example takes will depend entirely on your children and their level of concentration.

2. Move off around the available space, keeping close together, maybe creeping quietly, and look for the box containing the sea animals. Open it together and discuss the types of animals and how they would move – take as many ideas as possible from the children and then suggest that they could try moving in those ways. Our children were keen to explore the concept of moving through the waves using their bodies to stretch and arch, as illustrated by Figure 3.5.

3. Produce the blue material and fish to stimulate their imagination. Acting as a role model, encourage the children to use all parts of their body and to explore different levels. Some children might like to go under the material, many children will be making sea noises as they move

4. When it is time to move on, put an animal in the suitcase you are carrying with you. Then move on to find the next box. Maybe you could all shake as you go to get dry. Follow the same process, discuss the animals and how they might move, also find out what the children know about these animals – do they like to roll in the mud?

5. Explore these rolling, large, heavy actions with the group and then put an animal in the suitcase and move on, perhaps very slowly.

6. The next box contains the butterflies. Watch the children's suggested movements and then produce the ribbons on sticks. Explore the light whirling movements encouraging them to use all space and different levels. As before, put a butterfly in the suitcase when you have finished this activity.

Figure 3.5   These children are expressing through movement how an animal might move amongst the waves

7. Tell the group they are nearly at the end of their journey as you reach the suitcase full of materials. It's time to get dressed up and decorated and to dance at the party. Allow the children plenty of time to choose materials and dance – you could include instruments or use a CD player with some favourite music playing.

Stage three – recall the theme and develop a sequence
1. With the children sitting down on their spot, open the suitcase and take out the objects one by one. Ask the children to tell you how they moved on that part of their journey.

2. Stand up and put the sequence of movements together, talking the group through the adventure. You could also use appropriate pieces of music now or at a later stage.

Assessment opportunities

The practitioners would be able to take photographs of the different stages of the journey which the children could annotate and make into an individual book about their adventure. Observations of the children's participation would contribute to their developmental record.

Ways forward

Consider writing a story with the children about the journey and illustrate it in a variety of ways.

Introduce instruments to illustrate the journey.

Examples of activities starting from music (2)

Example 3D   Music activity

ACTIVITY PLAN

Theme:
▸ Exploring sound using percussion instruments.

Creative arts activity:
▸ Making percussion instruments with the children.

Why?
▸ Topic theme.

Suggested resources:
▸ A wide variety of different size and shaped containers.
▸ A selection of dried pulses, e.g. lentils, peas, beans.
▸ Buttons.
▸ Plastic film wrap, different types of paper (greaseproof, tissue).
▸ Elastic bands, sticky tape, gaffer tape, PVA glue.
▸ Shiny foil strips, sequins, material for decoration.
▸ Card, corrugated card.
▸ Coloured pens.
▸ World music selection to listen to.

Suggested questions to ask:
▸ What kind of sound does your instrument make?
▸ Why do the lentils sound different to the buttons?
▸ Can you play it loudly and/or quietly?
▸ How does your instrument make a sound?

Possible learning outcomes:
The children might:
▸ Capture experiences and responses with music.
▸ Explore and experience using a range of senses and movement.

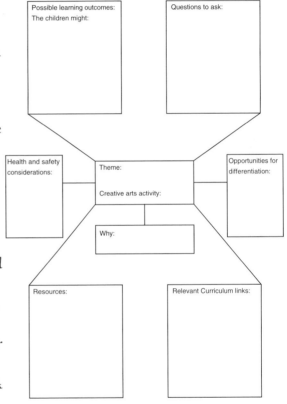

▶ Describe what they were trying to do.

▶ Begin to move to music, joining in with favourite songs.

▶ Explore and learn how sounds can be changed.

▶ Tap out simple repeated rhythms.

Opportunities for differentiation:

▶ Adult support for use of tape, scissors.

▶ Size of group.

Relevant curriculum links:

▶ KUW – use of materials.

▶ PSED – cultures and beliefs.

Health and safety considerations:

▶ Use of tools.

Exploration process

Stage one – introduce the theme

1. Remind the children about the instruments that you use in the setting and what you can do with them.

2. Look together at the available materials and suggest to the children that they might choose any they like to make their own musical instrument. The active involvement of a practitioner in this process, as shown by Figure 8 on the companion website, will encourage the children to have the confidence to try out unusual methods of making sounds. We did not have any real instruments for the children to look at because we wanted to see if they could use either recall or their own imagination.

Stage two – develop the theme

1. Play some catchy world music while the children are making their instruments. We found that it stimulated the children to investigate ways to play their instruments as they made them and developed their listening skills, as illustrated by Figure 3.6. It also promoted very positive peer group interaction.

2. Keep an open-ended idea about the type of instruments being made and let the individual children set the pace of the activity. Some children will be satisfied very quickly and some will stay focused for a long time, with something very particular in mind.

Figure 3.6   Listening to music while making instruments adds a new dimension to the task

Stage three – play the instruments

1. Listen to the sound that individual instruments make, encouraging the children to express an opinion about the instrument using relevant vocabulary. For example loud, quiet, fast, slow, high and low.

2. Choose some favourite songs to sing, accompanied by the instruments. You do not have to have them all playing at once but make sure everyone gets a turn. This one worked well:

> Old MacDonald had a farm
> E-I-E-I-O
> And on that farm he had some shakers
> E-I-E-I-O
> Shake shake here, shake shake there
> Here a shake, there a shake
> Everywhere a shake shake
> Old MacDonald had a farm
> E-I-E-I-O.

Carry on the song using all the different instruments.

Assessment opportunities

Observations on the children would clearly reveal stages of development and progress.

Photographs of the children playing their instruments would make a lovely book to share, and the music could be recorded to play back to the children.

Ways forward

Investigating the connection between sound and movement offers scope for further activities.

Example 3E   Movement and dance activity

ACTIVITY PLAN

Theme:
▶ The relationship between movement and sound.

Creative arts activity:
▶ Developing movements and sequences to respond to the sounds of percussion instruments.

Why?
▶ Follow-up on movements observed when children made their own instruments in a previous activity.

Suggested resources:
▶ Small, round, non-slip mats.
▶ Heavy-duty balloons with some lentils in them (one per child in group).
▶ A range of instruments. This activity would work equally well with bought instruments but is more relevant to the children if they have made and therefore have ownership of an instrument.
▶ Music to move to.

Suggested questions to ask:
▶ What sound does your instrument make?
▶ How do you play it?
▶ How can we move to that sound?
▶ Can we put the sounds together and make a dance?

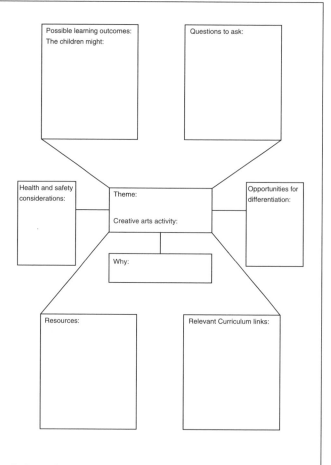

Possible learning outcomes: The children might:

Questions to ask:

Health and safety considerations:

Theme:

Creative arts activity:

Opportunities for differentiation:

Why:

Resources:

Relevant Curriculum links:

Possible learning outcomes:

The children might:

▶ Respond to sound with body movement.

▶ Imitate and create movement in response to music.

Opportunities for differentiation:

▶ Size of group.

▶ Choice of music.

Relevant curriculum links:

▶ CD – the balloons could be decorated with strips of foil, which would suggest a completely different movement.

▶ KUW – exploration of properties of air and balloons, materials.

Health and safety considerations:

▶ Floor surface.

Exploration process

Stage one – introduce the theme

1. Invite the children to choose an instrument or use one they have made and to sit down on one of the small mats.

2. Tell the children they are each going to have a turn playing their instrument and that everyone needs to listen carefully to the sound it makes because they are going to be thinking about how they could move to the sound.

3. Make sure that only one child at a time plays their instrument and as they do so encourage descriptive words from the children. For example, wriggly, shaky, and bumpy. We found that using the mats as a base really focused the children, as shown by Figure 3.7.

Stage two – develop the theme

1. Discuss with the children possible movements to accompany their instrument and try them out all together, still on their spot. Examples of movements would be shaking body parts, jumping, waving, clapping, nodding and rocking.

2. Remove the instruments and the spots and play some music for the children to move to, reminding them of the movements they have been exploring. Encourage use of space.

Figure 3.7   Working from their own space focused these children to concentrate and take turns

Stage three – develop a sequence

1. Get the children to stand in a circle on their mats.

2. Demonstrate putting some lentils into a strong balloon and blow it up. As you do this invite the children to pretend that they are a balloon being blown up, starting small and gradually expanding.

3. Demonstrate the sound the balloon makes and encourage the children to shake and rattle with the balloon.

4. Give each child a balloon and evolve a sequence of movements together. These might be:

    4 shakes up high
    4 shakes down low
    4 shakes side to side
    4 stamps.

5. Invite the children to move around the room, with you, developing their sequence. You could use appropriate music with a steady beat to accompany them.

Stage four – recall the theme

Encourage the children to choose an instrument, or a balloon, and to play and move with their instruments in an appropriate way, making good use of all the available space. You could try this with and without accompanying music and ask the children which they prefer.

Assessment opportunities

Practitioners could build up a set of photographs to demonstrate the movement sequence the children devised and there would be opportunities to make developmental observations on the children's progress.

Ways forward

As a problem solving activity children could make an instrument to illustrate a given sound or movement, for example the described sounds in *Peace at Last*, by Jill Murphy (Macmillan, 1995).

The expression of movement in a visual art form could be investigated.

Example 3F   Visual art activity

ACTIVITY PLAN

Theme:
▶ *Expressing movement.*

Creative arts activity:
▶ *Printmaking.*

Why?
▶ *Logical extension to use art materials, having explored movement through sound and dance.*

Suggested resources:
▶ *A table covered in plastic sheeting – this could be inside or outside.*
▶ *A drying rack that is easily accessible.*
▶ *Water-based block printing inks – these do produce a very different result to ready-mix paint.*
▶ *Rubber rollers (not sponge rollers).*
▶ *Paper for printmaking.*

Possible learning outcomes: The children might:

Questions to ask:

Health and safety considerations:

Theme:

Creative arts activity:

Opportunities for differentiation:

Why:

Resources:

Relevant Curriculum links:

▸ Paper taped onto the floor and also a big piece to work on on the floor.

▸ A selection of tools to explore – combs, toothbrushes, small plastering tools, toy cars, wooden and plastic clay tools, chopsticks, rubber snakes, we even used a child's slipper!

▸ Crayons, oil pastels.

▸ Protective aprons.

Suggested questions to ask:

▸ How can you use this tool?

▸ What colours can you see?

▸ What kind of marks are you making?

Possible learning outcomes:

The children might:

▸ Begin to combine movement, media or marks.

▸ Explore colour and begin to differentiate between colours.

▸ Differentiate marks and movement on paper.

Opportunities for differentiation:

▸ Time – there must be enough for children to explore possibilities.

▸ Adult support.

▸ Working on surfaces of different levels.

Relevant curriculum links:

▸ CLL – handwriting.

▸ KUW – materials.

Health and safety considerations:

▸ Use of tools.

Exploration process

Stage one – introduce the theme

1. Tape a long piece of plain paper onto the floor and invite the children to sit around the paper.

2. From an interesting-looking basket produce some printmaking tools. Pass them around the group to give the children a chance to hold and feel the tools that they will later be using. We used some music at this stage to make the whole experience more relaxed and to give practitioners the opportunity to observe what the children were doing with the tools.

3. Immediately the children will begin to use the rollers on the paper, as shown by Figure 9 on the companion website, and to explore what the other tools will

do to the paper, for example scoring the paper, mashing the paper. One of our children said, 'Will they make patterns? No, we need to use crayons'.

4. Introduce a variety of crayons or oil pastels and watch what the children do with them. Some might use them to draw around the tools, some might begin making their own patterns, while some of our children realised that the tools needed other media to make them work and began to mash the pastels up with the tools and to spread the colour, making a perfect introduction to the next part of the process.

5. Encourage the children to walk around the paper looking at all the patterns they can see.

Stage two – develop the theme

1. Work with a group of no more than four children around the plastic-covered table. Invite each child to choose a colour of the printing ink and squeeze out a small amount onto the plastic surface. We would suggest that the adult be in charge of the squeezing for obvious reasons!

2. Reintroduce the rubber rollers and encourage the children to roll over the ink. The children will make comments about the noise that the ink makes, and the way the shape spreads. You can then add more colours and observe the comments.

3. Introduce the tools and suggest the children see what kinds of marks they can make in the ink. Clearly this is going to be a messy process and the children will want to fully explore the inks, sometimes rolling them on their hands and making their own prints. It would be important to have established a set of ground rules so that the children know their boundaries.

4. Ensure that the children have quality uninterrupted time to explore the materials. This is a totally absorbing experience for children, the sensation of experiencing the different textures and moving fingers and tools through the inks to create their own special patterns. For many children this will be enough, but you might want to introduce the idea of taking a mono-print.

Stage three – extend the theme

Once a child has created a pattern on the table surface demonstrate how to carefully place a piece of paper on top of the ink and press down. When you gently peel the paper back the child will be amazed to see the pattern reproduced on the paper. Depending on the developmental stage of the child you might want to expand on this idea. We felt that while some children responded with excitement

Figure 3.8   This girl explored the process right to the end

to this development of the theme, for example the little girl illustrated by Figure 3.8, for many children the process was in itself an end result.

Assessment opportunities

Practitioners would be able to observe the progress of the children through the stages of the process and support those who were initially reluctant to become involved.

Ways forward

Practitioners might like to explore further types of simple printmaking; for example, building up a printing block or potato prints.

CHAPTER 4

Starting from movement and dance

This chapter will give you ideas of ways to develop movement and dance activities by:

- Highlighting the importance of movement and dance in the early years.
- Offering practical solutions to common concerns.
- Illustrating two dance activities each leading into an exploration of visual art and music.

Movement and dance is an activity that all young children naturally engage in as they play. Watch children, for example, in the role play area, in the book area or outside and you will notice a wide range of very individual and purposeful movements/dances taking place. Movement and dance are put together here because they are so inter-related that a sequence of movements could be called a dance.

Our role as practitioners is to build on what the children are showing us, developing skills such as responding to sound with body movement, beginning to move rhythmically and perhaps developing a repertoire of dances. This chapter will illustrate how an idea for a movement activity can unfold, develop existing skills and introduce new ideas which may then take the children into a new direction, to explore a different creative art form.

Movement and dance play an important role in developing creative awareness in young children in the following ways:

- They provide children with an alternative means of expressing emotions and feelings, giving them an opportunity to respond to others. This is particularly important for children with specific learning difficulties.

- They extend the children's vocabulary, embedding concepts such as high, low, under, behind, fast and slow.

- They encourage children to develop recall skills, through sequential pattern-making or telling a story.

- They can present children with a problem to solve, such as developing their own way to move like a spider or a tiger or even a dinosaur. It is quite an intellectual challenge to pretend to 'be' something else.

- They can demand the beginnings of cooperative work with peers.

- They are really good fun and invite children to enjoy moving and to find out what they can do with their bodies.

- They are an ideal way to introduce children to the wide variety of rhythms from around the world, ensuring that they appreciate the multi-cultural world they are growing up in.

It is clear that by regularly planning for movement and dance many other curricular areas would be enriched. However, many practitioners feel daunted by the prospect of managing such a session so the following may help allay some fears.

 DON'T PANIC IF...

I've got two left feet.
The movements that you will be doing are simple, repetitive and taken from natural body movements. You will be moving with the children, often copying their actions, and they will be too busy being in the dance to notice your performance.

I don't know what music to use.
There is a whole world of music out there and this is your opportunity to spend some time listening to it and deciding what would suit the activity best. The Resources section at the end of the book has some ideas to get you started, but as with many resources it works best if it is something that you like yourself because your enthusiasm will infect the children. Try to make sure that you use a wide range of music; it may be the only time in some children's lives that they hear, for example, jazz music.

I'm afraid they will go wild and I won't be able to control them.
They might, if you are not well prepared and do not have a structure to your session. Also you cannot suddenly offer the children a large space and not expect them to want to race around, so you need to build in opportunities for a free exploration of the area before you begin being more specific about your expectations. You will need to have a basic skeletal outline to the activity, which then allows you to incorporate the children's ideas.

I'm worried I won't keep their attention.
Don't make the session too long. All the activities described in the following chapter are divided into short stages, so depending on the maturity of the children you can decide how much you want the group to achieve.

My group is too big.
Spread the activity out over a week to make sure that the children receive the attention they need.

Space is a problem.
Again, consider how large the group needs to be and don't forget that movement and dance can just as easily take place outside.

The following two sections demonstrate ways in which movement and dance activities could lead into an exploration of other creative art forms.

Examples of activities starting from movement and dance (1)

Example 4A   Movement and dance activity

ACTIVITY PLAN

Theme:
▶ A journey into space.

Creative arts activity:
▶ Developing a sequence of movements that explore the idea of going into space.

Why?
▶ The idea came from the children following a music session.

Suggested resources:
▶ A large space to move in.
▶ A small round non-slip mat (e.g. a bath mat) for each child taking part in the activity.
▶ A big round shiny piece of material to represent the moon.
▶ A selection of cut-out star shapes.
▶ A silver ball – could be an ordinary ball painted silver.
▶ Ribbons on sticks, one per child.
▶ Appropriate music.
▶ A selection of coloured lengths of material.

Suggested questions to ask:
▶ What do we need to wear on our journey?
▶ What does this look like? (the moon)
▶ What does it feel like (the silver ball)
▶ How will s/he pass it on?
▶ What else do we see in the sky?

Possible learning outcomes: The children might:

Questions to ask:

Health and safety considerations:

Theme:

Creative arts activity:

Opportunities for differentiation:

Why:

Resources:

Relevant Curriculum links:

Suggested learning outcomes:

The children might:

▶ Respond to sound with body movement.

▶ Imitate and create movement in response to music.

▶ Begin to move rhythmically.

Opportunities for differentiation:

▶ Space – children not used to working in a group in a large space might need adult support.

▶ Structure – children who have already had opportunities to explore free play in a large space will be ready for a more structured activity.

Relevant curriculum links:

▶ KUW–time, place and communities–place.

▶ PD–health and bodily awareness.

Health and safety considerations:

▶ Floor surface, use of equipment.

Exploration process

Stage one – introduce the theme.

1. Arrange the mats in a circle on the floor and invite the children to come and sit on one.

2. Explain to the children that 'We are going to go on a long journey, up into space, to the moon. What do we need to do to get ready?' The children will respond with their own suggestions, which you must acknowledge and act on. For example our children were very anxious there would be enough food.

3. Ask 'What clothes will we need?' Put on your special boots – involve the children in actions such as pulling on the boots, shaking out the trousers, doing up the jackets.

4. On the spot shaking activity to get ready to go on the journey – shake different body parts to music.

Stage two – develop the theme

1. Start with the essential count-down to blast off!

2. Tell the children they are going to move in any way they like into space. When the music stops they will need to be on a different spot. Allow them some time

to explore moving to the music before they have to land, making sure that all adults are joining in too.

3. Children are sitting on a new mat. Ask, 'Now we have landed, where do you think we are?' Put the big shiny silver circle down and see what the children suggest. Our children were quick to tell us it was the moon.

4. Produce lots of silver stars and give at least one to each child. Introduce the idea of falling and shooting stars and encourage the children to twirl, whirl, high and low, with their stars, making good use of all the space. They could also explode, with high jumps. Music could be used here too.

5. Invite the children to place their stars on the moon shape, and return to their spot.

Stage three – calm it down.
1. Introduce the magic silver ball and tell the children you are going to pass it round the circle. As it gets to each child ask questions about it, for example is it hard or soft, heavy or light? Where do you think it came from? Make comments on what the individual children choose to do with it. For example, 'Can it float up high? You must be strong!' Some of our children decided to bowl it to each other, some children commented on their reflection in the ball, one little boy sat on it saying, 'It's gone!' This activity will give the children the opportunity to slow down, to relax and listen to each other but remember to consider the length of time children might have to wait for their turn with the ball if you have a large group with a high proportion of younger children in it.

Stage four – ending the journey
1. Ask the question, 'What else can we see in the sky?' You will get lots of answers but wait for the rainbow suggestion. Then give the children at least one ribbon on a stick each and encourage them to explore the idea of making a rainbow as illustrated by Figure 4.1, waving, twirling the ribbons as they come down to land on Earth. One little boy became very engrossed in the idea of wrapping the ribbon around his arm.

2. Provide a mixture of coloured materials for the children to lie down on and close their eyes. As they lie, recall the experience of the journey and allow for a short moment of quiet before the session ends.

Assessment opportunities

Practitioners will be able to make observations of individual children's responses to the challenges.

A group book of photographs would usefully show the sequence of the journey.

Figure 4.1   Using coloured ribbons on short sticks the children are exploring the concept of rainbows

Ways forward

- More developmentally able children could put the explored actions together to make a sequence.

- After our sessions we were interested in exploring further the idea of wrapping material.

Example 4B   Visual art activity

ACTIVITY PLAN

Theme:
▸ *Going on a journey.*

Creative arts activity:
▸ *Investigating string printing and properties of materials.*

Why?
▸ *Supports the idea of taking a journey already explored through dance; develops the possibilities of wrapping materials.*

Suggested resources:

▶ Large sheets of paper taped to the floor.
▶ A selection of drawing tools.
▶ A selection of pieces of string and wool, all different lengths.
▶ Paint in shallow containers.
▶ Pieces of string with a clothes peg clipped on to them.
▶ Paper for printing on.
▶ Lengths of different types of sticky tape – a useful tip is to pre-cut strips and place them on a plastic cutting board. The children can then peel them off as they need them.
▶ Lengths of pre-cut strips of coloured paper.
▶ Sticks or cardboard tubes.

Suggested questions to ask:

▶ Can you make your crayon follow the string?
▶ Can you drive your car along the pattern that you've made?

Possible learning outcomes:

The children might:
▶ Begin to combine movement, media or marks.
▶ Differentiate marks and movements on paper.
▶ Understand that different media can be combined to create new effects.

Opportunities for differentiation:

▶ A wide range of types of drawing tools to accommodate different gripping skills.
▶ Different levels to work on.

Relevant curriculum links:

▶ MD – length vocabulary.
▶ KUW – materials.

Health and safety considerations:

▶ Appropriate use of materials.

The diagram on the right contains the following boxes:

- Possible learning outcomes: The children might:
- Questions to ask:
- Health and safety considerations:
- Theme:
- Creative arts activity:
- Opportunities for differentiation:
- Why:
- Resources:
- Relevant Curriculum links:

Exploration process

Stage one – introduce the theme

1. Invite the children to sit around the paper on the floor, giving them pieces of string and wool to arrange on the paper. Allow time for exploration of the patterns that they make with the materials, commenting on them. For example, 'I

can see your pattern looks like a snail's shell and yours looks like a long, long road.' Encourage the children to talk to each other about the shapes they have made.

2. Remind the group they are thinking about going on a journey, introduce the drawing tools and suggest that they could make the crayon go on a journey by following the string pattern they have just made, as shown by the little boy in Figure 10 on the companion website. Some children will need to be encouraged to press harder or introduce tools like felt-tip pens if they are having difficulty applying enough pressure. See if they can fill up all the paper with different 'journey patterns'.

3. Introduce the strips of sticky tape and watch what the children do with them, commenting on and developing their ideas. We saw children sticking the tape straight on to the paper to make new roads, as well as sticking the tape over the string.

4. Provide strips of paper of different colours and you will observe the children using these in a variety of ways. One little girl, illustrated in Figure 11 on the companion website, used her string and tape to make a lead for her small toy rabbit, which she then took for a walk around the paper! Some children drove the toy cars over the paper, developing the journey theme further by drawing houses and petrol stations to visit.

Stage two – develop the theme
1. Set up a table with the paint, string and paper, and in small groups introduce the skill of string printing by providing each child with a length of string and a clothes peg to clip on to it. This in itself could be an interesting challenge for some children.

2. Demonstrate how to dip the string, whilst holding the clothes peg, into a chosen colour of paint. Children will comment on the change of string colour and some will really explore just the process of swirling the string around in the container. Suggest that the string could be dragged over the paper to make patterns and encourage the children to talk about what they can see as they do this. All the children we worked with found this a totally exciting experience, as Figure 4.2 illustrates.

3. Introduce the idea of folding the paper in half, putting the string which has been dipped in the paint inside the paper and gently pulling the string out, leaving a trail of paint as it comes out. Open the paper and look at the pattern. One of our group discovered that if they dipped the string in water it diluted the paint and changed the effect.

Figure 4.2   The process of string printing offers a complete sensory experience

4. You could add PVA glue to the paint to thicken it or use acrylic paint and produce a much more textural appearance. Remember that the process is the important experience and that some children may not be interested in the technique of the printing.

Stage three – extend the theme
1. Reintroduce the string and wool along with strips of pre-cut material, strips of plastic, ribbons. Don't make the strips too long or they become unmanageable. Provide sticks, cardboard rolls or anything which children could wind the materials around.

2. Invite the children to explore the materials on the table and watch what they do. The children we worked with became engrossed in the process of wrapping layers of materials, sticking them securely with the strips of sticky tape. There were many opportunities to discuss colours and texture.

Some children will be satisfied with the process and some may like to turn their wrapped object into a puppet or whatever their imagination dictates. It is necessary to have an adult, who will be able to make extensive observations on the child's progress, available to support this process.

3. Display the stages of the exploration process for the children to share with each other and their families.

Assessment opportunities

Photographs will remind children about the process and encourage them to recall the experience.

The activity provides opportunities to observe children's fine motor skills and levels of focused attention on a given task.

Ways forward

■ The practitioners in our sessions were aware that some children were developing the idea of wrapping materials in their role play, for example by wrapping dolls up, and this could be explored further. It might also be possible to bring some music into the theme.

Example 4C   Music activity

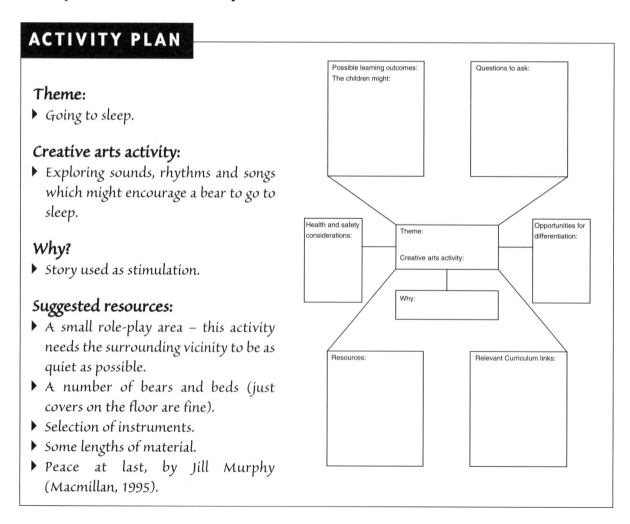

ACTIVITY PLAN

Theme:
▶ Going to sleep.

Creative arts activity:
▶ Exploring sounds, rhythms and songs which might encourage a bear to go to sleep.

Why?
▶ Story used as stimulation.

Suggested resources:
▶ A small role-play area – this activity needs the surrounding vicinity to be as quiet as possible.
▶ A number of bears and beds (just covers on the floor are fine).
▶ Selection of instruments.
▶ Some lengths of material.
▶ Peace at last, by Jill Murphy (Macmillan, 1995).

Possible learning outcomes: The children might:

Questions to ask:

Health and safety considerations:

Theme:

Creative arts activity:

Opportunities for differentiation:

Why:

Resources:

Relevant Curriculum links:

Suggested questions to ask:
▶ How do you get to sleep at night?
▶ Why do we need to sleep?
▶ What things might keep you awake?

Possible learning outcomes:
The children might:
▶ Begin to move to music, listen to or join in rhymes or songs.
▶ Respond to sound with body movement.
▶ Show an interest in the way musical instruments sound.

Opportunities for differentiation:
▶ A range of instruments.
▶ Adult support.

Relevant curriculum links:
▶ CLL – make up own story.
▶ KUW – materials, what would feel soft?

Health and safety considerations:
▶ Number of children in space.

Exploration process

Stage one – introduce the theme

1. At group story time read the story using a wide range of visual aids, including the bears and lanterns (you could have made these with the children). Allow time to discuss the implications of the story and for children to express their own experiences of this situation.

2. Make a list with the children of all the things that might help the little bear to get to sleep. Tell the children that they are going to turn the role-play area into the bear's cave and explore some of these ideas.

3. Fully involve the children in this process, keeping the area quite basic without too many distractions. (We set up four bears in their cosy beds, lots of cushions and soft wrapping materials. We also included some lullabies on pieces of card and storybooks.) Agree with the children that a limited number of children at a time will be able to explore this role-play area but that they will all get a turn.

Stage two – develop the theme

1. Work with small groups of children, they need a bear with a bed each. Tell the children that all methods of getting the bears to sleep have failed and now they

Figure 4.3 **These girls are really focused on the task of getting the bears to go to sleep**

are going to try using musical instruments to lull them to sleep. First make sure that each bear is well tucked up in bed.

2. Introduce a range of instruments to the group, including loud and quiet instruments. Encourage each child to individually play an instrument, to all listen to the sound it makes and discuss if this sound would be appropriate to encourage sleep. The practitioner needs to comment on and develop the children's vocabulary. Having discarded the noisy instruments, encourage the children to choose an instrument to play to their bear. At this point you can also model a quiet voice when talking to the children and they will copy this when telling their bears that it's time to go to sleep.

3. Observe the children, for example, as in Figure 4.3 as they play their instruments, commenting on patterns that you like and the actions they are making. For example, using the beater very gently, shaking the bells very slowly. Encourage the children to explore all the instruments but don't let this session run for too long or they will lose concentration.

Stage three – conclude the theme
1. Tell the children the bears are so nearly asleep but that they need to be wrapped up in some materials and rocked gently while the children sing a lullaby to them.

Modelling a quiet, gentle movement, support the children while they wrap a chosen piece of material around their bear.

2. Choose a favourite lullaby and sing it together, accompanying it yourself with one of the instruments. Remember the voice is an instrument too and the children could be reminded that they are choosing to make their voices quiet so as not to startle the bear. Encourage the children to rock their bear as they sing, keeping a slow and steady rhythm and movement.

3. Close the session by asking the children to carefully put the bears into their beds and tiptoe out of the role-play area.

Assessment opportunities

Working with a small group of children at a time will ensure that the practitioner is able to observe stages of development and any significant areas of progress.

Ways forward

Expressive movements could be encouraged through a movement and dance sequence.

Examples of activities starting from music and dance (2)

Example 4D   Movement and dance activity

ACTIVITY PLAN

Theme:
▶ *Travelling and exploring.*

Creative arts activity:
▶ *Explorers' dance, developing into a sequence.*

Why?
▶ *Dinosaur topic.*

Suggested resources:
▶ *Round mats – one per child.*
▶ *Large space – could be outside.*
▶ *Appropriate music.*
▶ *Plastic toy animals, e.g. a dinosaur, a tiger and an elephant.*

Suggested questions to ask:

▸ What will we need on our journey?

▸ What might we see on our journey?

▸ How will you feel?

Suggested learning outcomes:

The children might:

▸ Respond to sound with body movement.

▸ Imitate and create movement in response to music and imagination.

▸ Develop a sequence of movements linked to an idea.

Opportunities for differentiation:

▸ Size of group.

▸ Adult support.

Relevant curriculum links:

▸ CLL – stories and rhymes about exploration. For example, *Walking through the Jungle*, by Julie Lacome (Walker Books, 1995).

▸ KUW – living things, bones, telescope.

▸ PSED – self-care.

▸ CD – looking at artists' work, Rousseau.

Health and safety considerations:

▸ Floor surface.

Possible learning outcomes: The children might:		Questions to ask:
Health and safety considerations:	**Theme:** **Creative arts activity:** **Why:**	Opportunities for differentiation:
Resources:		Relevant Curriculum links:

Exploration process

Stage one – introduce the theme

1. Invite the children to sit on their spot in a big circle and explain that they are all going to go on a journey during which time they might find some dinosaur bones or some wild animals.

2. Get ready for the journey – What will we need? As the children make suggestions, demonstrate different movements, for example as shown by Figure 4.4, as they wriggle on their socks or stretch their arms into their jumpers. Encourage movements that include sitting and standing.

3. Pack the rucksacks. Again, ask the children for suggestions. Food will certainly feature and you could include movements such as screwing the cap on the water bottle. Don't forget the hats and sunscreen, which they could first put on their bodies.

4. Introduce a telescope and discuss what it could be used for. Practise extending it out and pushing it in, to make sure it is working properly. Maybe they could look at the person next to them through their telescope, as the boy shown in Figure 4.5 is doing very earnestly.

Figure 4.4   Getting ready to explore the jungle

Figure 4.5   It's very important to be able to use a telescope when looking for wild animals

5. Practise walking and looking through the telescope by creating a short sequence, as follows: 4 steps on the spot followed by 4 stretching out the telescope movements – these could go up, down or to the side.

6. Introduce some slow, steady beat music for the children and adults to move to in this sequence.

7. The children return to their own spot to finish this stage – it's time to have a drink from the water bottle.

Stage two – develop the theme

1. Introduce the plastic dinosaur to the children and tell them you have found a huge dinosaur bone and it is very heavy. Model holding and lifting this heavy imaginary bone. Encourage the children to stand up and pass this bone to each other making sure you praise their actions to help develop the relevant vocabulary.

2. Invite the children to stand up and introduce a sequence of lifting a heavy bone, all together to the count of 4 to lift it and 1 to drop it as it is so heavy.

3. Discuss how a dinosaur with bones this big and heavy might move.

4. Develop a slow, heavy, steady beat dinosaur dance with the children, using suitable music. Encourage good use of space and working at different levels.

5. When this stage reaches a natural conclusion encourage the children to slowly sink back on their spots.

Stage three – extend the theme

1. Introduce the plastic tiger to the children, discuss its name and any information the children may offer about it. Develop the idea of the tiger creeping stealthily forward through the jungle.

2. Tell the children they are going to look for a tiger and remind them of their explorers' dance, using the telescope. You can then develop a sequential dance that is as simple or complicated as your group can cope with. The following example is the one we used with our group, keeping to a steady beat of 4 counts. It is a good idea to repeat the movements several times before you introduce any music.

Marching to 4 counts
Lunging with the telescope in different directions to 4 counts
Feet staying on floor, creep hands forward for 4 counts
Feet staying on floor, creep hands backwards for 4 counts
Tiptoe low down for 4 counts
Tiptoe, stretching up high for 4 counts
March around the space pushing aside the jungle foliage to finish the sequence.

3. Divide the group into two and invite each group to show the other group their sequence. Remind them of the creeping action of the tiger and ask where this features in their dance.

4. Return to the circle for a well-deserved drink and snack from the rucksacks.

Assessment opportunities

Practitioners are able to observe children's participation, actions and ideas.

A book of photographs will describe and record the adventure and encourage children to recall the experience.

Ways forward

The children could develop musical instruments to accompany the explorers' dance.

It would be easy to introduce other animals into the activity, for example an elephant, and discuss how the movements would be different.

The theme of bones, stones, and other things that are dug up offers potential for development.

Example 4E   Visual art activity

ACTIVITY PLAN

Theme:
▶ Bones and stones.

Creative arts activity:
▶ Exploring clay.

Why?
▶ Development of a dinosaur theme.
▶ Searching for hidden objects.

Suggested resources:
▶ Clay, red and white if possible. (We would recommend that you use proper clay not air-hardening clay. You will not be firing this and will be able to recycle and reuse it, unless it dries out completely.)
▶ Large builder's tray.
▶ Water.
▶ Clay tools.
▶ Mark-making equipment.

Possible learning outcomes: The children might:

Questions to ask:

Health and safety considerations:

Theme:

Creative arts activity:

Opportunities for differentiation:

Why:

Resources:

Relevant Curriculum links:

▸ Table protection and A4 size pieces of cardboard for children to work on.

▸ A selection of stones, sticks, shells and bones if available and clean.

▸ Plastic dinosaurs/animals.

Suggested questions to ask:

▸ What does it look like?

▸ How does it feel?

▸ What can you find?

Possible learning outcomes:

▸ The children might:

▸ Be interested in and describe the texture of things.

▸ Differentiate marks and movements on paper.

▸ Create three-dimensional structures.

▸ Experiment to create different textures.

Opportunities for differentiation:

▸ Size of group.

▸ A variety of levels on which to work.

▸ Adult support.

Relevant curriculum links:

▸ KUW – materials

▸ PD – use of tools.

▸ CD – looking at sculptors' work.

Health and safety considerations:

▸ Use of tools.

Exploration process

Stage one – introduce the theme

1. Invite the children to sit in a circle around a large piece of paper taped to the floor. Show the children an interesting-looking stone and describe why you like it, what you have noticed about it. Tell them where it came from – out of the ground, maybe in your garden.

2. Pass a selection of items around the circle so that each child has something to look at. Invite the children to use all their senses, to see how the item looks, feels, smells, does it make a sound and would they want to taste it?

3. Ensure that each child has the opportunity to talk about their object, at all times be supportive and encouraging and allow for the child to follow what may seem an obscure link in their imagination.

4. Encourage the children to explore other objects, and use the mark-making tools to visually describe what they can see on the big piece of paper. We found that children quickly observed patterns and shapes. Very few children used the objects to draw around and if they did we encouraged them to make a bigger one around the little one, to make a 'house' for it. Discuss what might have made the holes in the stones and shells and how the sticks came to be such strange shapes.

5. Stand back and look at the picture. Most children will be able to identify their own work. This will make a great display, with photos and children's comments alongside the natural objects.

Stage two – develop the theme

1. Provide a small group of children with a builder's tray (mixing spot) in which there is a little water and a selection of pieces of clay. You do not need much. This is going to give them the opportunity to discover the properties of clay in a play situation. It is important that an adult is present to be able to support and observe the children's comments.

2. Encourage the children to squeeze and spread the clay, as illustrated by Figure 4.6, to describe how it feels and to notice what happens when it mixes with the water.

Figure 4.6   Children will naturally engage in conversation whilst exploring the qualities of clay

3. When they have had sufficient time, suggest they might like to hide some stones, shells or sticks in the clay, adding more clay or water if necessary. Dinosaurs could also be part of this play if required. We used them because we were developing a theme about dinosaurs, but you could use any animals.

4. At all times listen to, repeat and extend the children's textural vocabulary. This type of exploration may be as much as some children need and they may need it frequently before they are ready for the next stage.

Stage three – extend the theme

1. Provide a small group of children with a ball of clay, which is not too sticky. Have available the stones and sticks to look at as they work. Encourage the children to push fingers into the clay to make holes, maybe like they can see in the stones. See if they can squeeze the clay to make shapes like the natural objects and then use the clay tools to copy the marks and patterns on them. A garlic press is great fun for making wiggly worm shapes. Remind them how the use of added water will smooth the clay and moisten it if it is getting too dry.

2. The clay objects could be saved as part of a natural landscape for small world play. Once dried, they will eventually crack with use but that can be another opportunity to observe the properties of materials. If the budget is an issue and if the clay has not completely dried out, it can be squeezed back into a big ball and covered with a damp cloth or put in a covered bucket with a little water in it, to be used another time. Most children at this stage are happy for the experience to be the important part as long as the adults are not demanding an end result.

Stage four – investigating another property of clay

1. Provide each child with a small ball of clay and show them how to flatten it slightly with a rolling pin.

2. Have a selection of items which the child can use to press into the clay and observe the impression it leaves when taken out.

3. Encourage the children to explore their environment with their ball of clay and see what patterns they can find. Our children discovered that practically anything they pressed their clay onto made a pattern and some children actually then referred back to the drawing patterns they had made earlier.

Assessment opportunities

Practitioners can observe language and physical skills.

A photographic record can be made of the children's work, and they can be encouraged to draw their creations.

Ways forward

There are opportunities to develop impression work by using a variety of materials, such as playdough, or plasticine, to make moulds.

Language skills may be developed, as we found the children in our sessions clearly identified opposites like smooth, bumpy, dry and wet.

Further activities might develop sand and malleable materials play.

Example 4F   Music activity

ACTIVITY PLAN

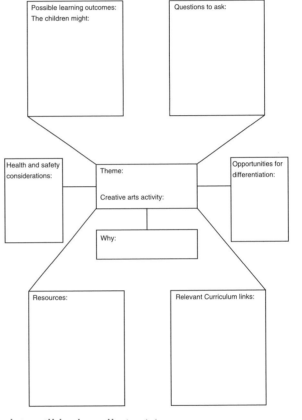

Theme:
▶ Opposites.

Creative arts activity:
▶ To investigate opportunities to explore opposites using musical instruments.

Why?
▶ To develop an idea from a previous experience.

Suggested resources:
▶ Dinosaur Roar!, by Paul and Henrietta Stickland (Ragged Bears, 1997).
▶ Cloth 1, with instruments that will make a loud and short sound: for example, a drum, claves, tambourine, coconut, woodblock.
▶ Cloth 2, with instruments that will make a quiet and long sound: for example, Indian bells, triangle, cymbal, xylophone.
▶ If you can, use bright multi-cultural material, it will look really inviting.
▶ Selection of beaters to produce loud or quiet sounds.
▶ Home-made or toy dinosaurs.

Suggested questions to ask:
▶ Is it loud or quiet?
▶ Do they sound the same?
▶ How shall we decide when to stop?
▶ Listen to our voices – are they high or low?

Possible learning outcomes:
The children might:
▶ Show an interest in the way musical instruments sound.
▶ Tap out some simple repeated rhythms and make some up.

▶ Explore and learn how sounds can be changed.

▶ Explore the different sounds of instruments.

Opportunities for differentiation:

▶ Group size.

▶ Adult support.

▶ Types of instruments offered.

Relevant curriculum links:

▶ CLL – storytelling.

▶ KUW – use of materials.

▶ MD – counting opportunities.

Health and safety considerations:

▶ Use of instruments.

Exploration process

Stage one – introduce the theme

1. Read *Dinosaur Roar!* to the children. Take opportunities to encourage the children to make connections between the size of the dinosaur and the type of noise it might make.

2. We had made dinosaurs with the children and they sang a welcome song to them, making them dance. You could use a variety of toy dinosaurs for the same purpose. We ensured that we praised the children, saying 'Well done, you really moved to the rhythm of that song.'

3. Leave the dinosaurs in a safe place for future use.

Stage two – develop the theme

1. Invite the children to sit around cloth 1, with the loud and short sounding instruments, telling them they are going to listen to the sounds that the instruments can make. At this stage introduce a signal that means stop – for example, one hand raised, palm facing the children.

2. Encourage each child to choose an instrument and explore the sound – when they have had sufficient time, try the 'stop' signal. Tell the children that, like one of the dinosaurs in the story, they are going to try to make a loud and short sound with their instrument. Because you have pre-selected the available instruments this concept will not appear too confusing.

Figure 4.7   An interesting selection of instruments stimulates children to focus on a task

3. Going around the circle, as shown in Figure 4.7, encourage children to play their loud and short sound. As they do so tell them the name of the instrument if they don't already know it and ask the other children if the sound is correct.

4. If you feel the children are developmentally ready, you can play a game called 'Pass the sound'. The children will have to watch to see when it is their turn to play as they pass the sound around the circle, and for some children this will be quite a challenge. Allow several opportunities to do this, encouraging children to change instruments and try something different. Keep reminding them about the loud and short concept. We noticed that many children were able to develop the ability to make a louder sound with practice and improving self-confidence.

Stage three – change the opposites
1. Invite the children to sit around cloth 2, with the quiet and long sounding instruments on it. Explain that they are going to listen first and play in a moment.

2. Tell the children you are going to play the Indian bells and you want them to count and see what number they reach when they can no longer hear the sound. It works better if an adult plays the bells for the first time to ensure that you get a good, long quality of sound. Model the steady counting with the children.

3. Repeat the previous example with the children, passing the quiet long sound. The example of Figure 12 on the companion website illustrates clearly the level of concentration of the group we worked with.

Stage four – add a challenge and recall the theme

1. Invite each child to choose an instrument from either selection and remove the rest. Ask them if they can find a way of changing the sound of the instrument. This may be by scratching a tambourine rather than banging it or by scraping a guiro rather than tapping it. Beaters covered in different materials will also produce a different effect. Observe and comment on the children's approach to this task, making sure they show each other what they have discovered.

2. Remind the children about the dinosaur story and suggest they might like to use their instruments to make up a dinosaur dance. For example, the children who chose to play loud short sounds could march or jump as they played and the children who chose quiet long sounds could wriggle or float as they played. Don't forget to remind them about the 'stop' command! You could also add music at this stage.

Assessment opportunities

Practitioners can observe the approach to the given task and the use of cooperative skills.

These could be the opportunity to record the different sounds the children have discovered.

Ways forward

The children could develop simple musical compositions using symbols to represent the type of sound.

The 'Pass the sound' game can be made more challenging by introducing the rule that if someone plays the sound twice, it then has to be passed in the opposite direction.

Children could make their own instruments to display different sound qualities.

Integrated arts planning format

The completed activity records here show how the projects described in this book link together. A blank photocopiable is also included for practitioners to use in recording how the projects in their own settings are integrating.

Visual art activity (2A)

Theme: Pathways

Art activity: Exploration of materials

An installation activity that encourages children to explore a variety of different materials and experiences.

Movement and dance activity (2B)

Theme: Going on a bear hunt

MD activity: Exploring dramatic movement

In using a familiar story the children are encouraged explore a range of movements and work cooperatively.

Music activity (2C)

Theme: Going on a bear hunt

Music activity: Exploration of qualities of instruments, including the voice

The children explore sounds to interpret parts of the story and build up a sequence sound story.

Visual art activity (2D)

Theme: Insects

Art activity: Using materials to create and decorate

An installation activity that encourages children to explore structures and creative use of materials.

Movement and dance activity (2E)

Theme: Stars

MD activity: Developing movement to interpret a story

Individually and cooperatively exploring movements to illustrate a favourite story.

Music activity (2F)

Theme: Stars

Music activity: Identification of musical sounds and beginnings of composition

Exploration of sound and possibilities of working with a partner.

Chapter 2   Starting from the visual arts

Music activity (3A)

Theme: Going on a musical journey

Music activity: Exploration of sound

Following an exploration of instruments, the children use an outdoor area to investigate the sounds they can hear.

➡

Visual art activity (3B)

Theme: Insects

Visual art activity: Exploration of light and shadow

Children explore shadow possibilities using light boxes and a range of materials.

➡

Movement and dance activity (3C)

Theme: Going to journey

MD activity: A sequential journey in movement and dance

The children experience the fun of going on a journey, discovering items on the way and building up a sequential pattern of movement.

Music activity (3D)

Theme: Exploring sound using percussion instruments

Music activity: Making percussion instruments

The children explore a range of materials to make and use instruments.

➡

Movement and dance activity (3E)

Theme: The relationship between movement and sound

MD activity: Responding to sounds of percussion instruments

The children will explore movements to the sounds made by home-made instruments.

➡

Visual art activity (3F)

Theme: Expressing movement

Visual art activity: Printmaking

The children investigate printmaking tools and explore the process.

Chapter 3   Starting from music

Movement and Dance activity (4A)

Theme: A journey into space

MD activity: Developing a sequence of movements

The children explore movement possibilities based on a journey into space.

⇨

Visual art activity (4B)

Theme: Going on a journey

Visual art activity: String printing

The children can investigate the properties of materials and explore the process of printing with string.

⇨

Music activity (4C)

Theme: Going to sleep

Music activity: Exploration of sounds, rhythms and song

The children explore the instruments to make appropriate sounds to soothe teddy bears to sleep.

Movement and Dance activity (4D)

Theme: Travelling and exploring

MD activity: Developing a dance sequence

Using a story as a stimulus the children develop a dance to represent the idea of an explorer in a jungle.

⇨

Visual art activity (4E)

Theme: Bones and stones

Visual art activity: Exploring clay

The children have the opportunity to investigate a range of natural objects and develop the process of working with clay.

⇨

Music activity (4F)

Theme: Opposites

Music activity: Exploration of opposites using musical instruments

Using a story as a stimulus the children explore making opposite sounds with instruments.

Chapter 4   Starting from movement and dance

97

Visual arts

Paint and mark-making tips

- Explore different types of paint (non-toxic) such as acrylic, watercolours and inks. Remember you can mix things like washing-up liquid, washing powder, sand, glue and vegetable oil with most types of paint to thicken it and make it more stimulating.

- Paint on flat and upright surfaces as the paint responds in different ways. Try painting on windows, clear Perspex, thick polythene sheets, bubble wrap, material.

- Use paint inside and outside to explore scale opportunities.

- Experiment with different tools to apply paint, such as big and small brushes, twigs, cotton buds, cloths, sponges, string, fingers and feet.

- Good ideas for mark-making are oil pastels, chalk pastels, felt-tip pens, graphite pencils.

Light and shadow tips

- Explore a variety of light sources – torches, overhead projector, slide projector, lamps, sun.

- Test out different fabrics and papers to make the screen for a light box e.g. cotton, Lycra, tracing paper, silk. Try coloured materials, too.

- Project anything that will cast an interesting shadow – Christmas tree decorations, household objects.

- Explore on a big and small scale using small light boxes and large pieces of sheeting. Play games – guess who/what is making the shadow.

Print tips

- Mono-printing: use water-based printing inks. Roll the ink onto a hard surface and make marks into this with a variety of tools.

- Oil printing: print with vegetable cooking oil onto paper, experiment with foam blocks, feathers, string. Let the print dry a little then rub powder paint into the oil.

- Potato prints: still wonderful, but try a variety of paints and surfaces to print on.

Clay

- Use real clay, red or white, but not air-hardening clay which has added fibres and is hard to manipulate. Buy bags from educational suppliers: it's cheap and will last a long time if looked after. Store it in a bucket with a lid on to keep it damp.

- Use a piece of cardboard to work on to stop the clay sticking to a table-top. You can use a variety of tools, for example strong plastic cutlery, garlic press and combs, to explore the properties of the clay.

Materials/natural objects

- Weaving materials can include strips of coloured bin liners, coloured plastic bags, thick wool, string rope, ribbons.

- Natural objects such as shells, stones and sticks to make patterns.

Sources of supplies

- Remainder stock shops ('pound shops').

- DIY stores.

- Stationers.

- Army surplus stores for items such as big foil sheets, tape, plastic sheets, tents, parachutes.

- Fabric shops and market stalls.

- Educational supplies catalogues.

- Kitchen suppliers.

- Charity shops.

- Art and craft stores.

- Scrapstores.

- Free from families and local companies in the community.

ARTISTS' FURTHER RESOURCES SUGGESTIONS

Damm, Antje (2005) *Ask Me*. London: Frances Lincoln Publishers.
Gee, T. *A Moveable Feast – a Workshop Handbook*, www.themoveablefeast.co.uk (accessed September 2006).
Van Swaaij, L. and Klare, J. (2000) *The Atlas of Experience* (trans. D. Winner). London: Bloomsbury.

Music

Most music-making in the Early Years should involve singing and rhythmic work using hand-held un-tuned percussion instruments. These are instruments that produce a rhythm rather than a tune. However, many children of nursery and reception age are ready and have the enthusiasm to experiment with tonal instruments such as xylophones and electronic keyboards.

Essential range of instruments

- Hand-held percussion suitable for Early Years children, such as egg shakers, claves, tambourines, tambours, maracas, triangles, Indian bells, sleigh bells, small drums, woodblocks, agogos. It is highly recommended that you buy high quality instruments, fewer if necessary, rather than a lot of cheaper plastic instruments.

- Several tuned instruments, such as the little xylophones that are readily commercially available that have coloured keys, enabling the children to invent a tune and recall it by a pattern of colours.

Desirable additions to your range of instruments

A range of 'real' instruments is desirable, some examples of which follow, reflecting the richness and diversity of our culture. These can be ordered from general educational suppliers or local music shops. Consider the cultures that are represented in your setting and ask for advice from the families:

Mbira (African thumb piano)
Djembe (African drums)
Darabuka (Middle East and North African drums)
Panpipes
Electronic keyboards.

New ideas

Keep a look out for new developments in musical resources, as they are constantly evolving. For example, Boom-Wackers are tuned plastic tubes which can be beaten on different surfaces to produce single notes, chords and patterns. They are a particularly effective way to draw boys into music-making because they involve large-scale movement to create sounds. These and related music resources are available through mainstream educational suppliers and good music shops.

Make your own instruments

Ensure you keep a well-stocked range of items to enable children to explore the possibilities of making their own instruments to produce a required sound. These will include card tubes, plastic film wrap, dried pulses and sticks. It is also well worth exploring the shops at specific times of the year, for example just after Easter time, as you can find reduced plastic egg containers to make into simple egg shakers.

Record your music

Make sure you have a reasonably good quality cassette player or similar to enable the children to record their music-making. Don't forget that many mobile phones will record sound.

You will also need an extensive range of different types of music for the children to listen to. We would recommend that young children are not automatically exposed to 'background' music all day long because they begin to lose the ability to really listen to a piece of music, which is a skill in itself.

ARTISTS' FURTHER RESOURCES SUGGESTIONS

Hedger, A. (n.d.) *Hubble-Bubble: 22 New Things to Do in Music Sessions with the Very Young*. Golden Apple Productions, a division of Chester Music Limited.
Hedger, A. (n.d.) *New Ways with Old Rhymes: 21 Rhymes with Singing and Percussion Activities*. Golden Apple Publications, a division of Chester Music Limited.
Floyd, M. (1991) *Folk Songs from Africa*. London: Faber Music.
Gritton, P. and Bolam, K. (1993) *Folk songs from the Caribbean*. London: Faber Music.
Both the latter collections have an accompanying cassette or CD. As well as the lyrics and music they also include simple percussion activities.

Movement and dance

Movement and dance does not need very much in the way of resources but one important thing is space. Most Early Years settings have a dedicated outside space divided up into areas that contain fixed items, for example a sandpit, a garden or planting area and shed for wheeled toys storage. While these are all an important part of delivering the Early Years curriculum it could be worthwhile thinking about the space carefully before items are 'fixed' because an area can sometimes be more versatile with a little more flexibility. The following are some points that may influence your decision.

The **advantages of an empty space** are:

- It ensures the children focus on the activity, as there is nothing else to distract them.

- The children are able to safely create big energetic movements in a controlled area without the threat of hurting themselves or others.

- Music can be played loudly if appropriate.

The **disadvantages of a large empty space** are that it can have the opposite effect of dissipating the focus, especially with only a few children in it. This can be addressed by cordoning off one area and then working the group in a circle to direct the energy inwards.

An empty space means that the practitioner has to be really prepared with dance ideas and must use resources to stimulate the children. If the children are not engaged in an activity they can cause havoc by endlessly racing around, which is a potentially stressful and non-productive situation for a practitioner to be in. It is also bad practice to get everyone warmed up and then run out of ideas and have to ask them to sit down again and get cold.

Materials

- Small non-slip bath mats are a brilliant idea, as illustrated in many of the activity examples, because they provide the children with a place to 'be', which also helps to focus their concentration.

- A range of beautiful materials will help stimulate movement. One tip is to sew a little sand in a corner of a lightweight piece of material, which will alter the way it moves.

- Ribbons and scarves – these can be hand-held, tied on short sticks or sewn onto a small hair scrunchie and then placed on a finger or wrist. These can be used for a variety of large movement and pattern explorations.

Music

Music is an important resource and you need to set aside a significant amount of time to listen to a selection and research your collection. Choose tracks that really do what you want them to do, for example, create an atmosphere, provide a heavy beat or complex rhythm. Listen out for music and if you hear something you like – on television, radio, in the cinema or out shopping – find out the name of the artist.

The following are some music ideas to start from. Please check all lyrics before use to ensure they are age-appropriate, and, if necessary, clear copyright with the appropriate copyright-holder.

- **Electronic dance music:**

  Mylo

  The Chemical Brothers

  Lemon Jelly

  Orbital

  Fat Boy Slim

- **Traditional world music:**

  Regional UK folk

  Blue Grass/American folk

  Cuban rhythms

  Flamenco rhythms

  African /Indian drumming/singing

- **Film scores:**

  Disney/Pixel films

  Bollywood films

  Quentin Tarantino soundtracks

- **Compilation CDs:**

  Music from adverts

  Music from films

  Music from television programmes

  Compilation CDs given free with newspapers

- **Music websites** – some online music websites allow you to listen to a short sample of the album so you can try before you buy.

- **Apple: iTunes Music Store** – a large catalogue of songs in digital formats available for purchase and download.

  www.apple.com/itunes/music

- **Amazon.com Music** – online shopping for thousands of music CDs.

  www.amazon.com

- **Music companies**:

  Jabadoo

  www.jabadoo.org

  Bare Toed (Early Years movement, play and dance)

  www.baretoed.co.uk

- **Dance organisations**

  - www.danceuk.org

  - www.communitydance.org.uk

  - www.ndta.org.uk (The National Dance Teachers Association)

  - www.akademi.co.uk (South Asian Dance in the UK)

  - www.adad.org.uk (Association of Dance of the African Diaspora)

ARTISTS' FURTHER RESOURCES SUGGESTIONS

Dance Books Ltd – www.dancebooks.co.uk
Specialist dance bookshop that sells new books, videos and CDs.
Sightlines Initiative – www.sightlines-initiative.com
Supports creative thinking and practice in early childhood services across the UK.

INDEX

Added to the page number 'f' denotes a figure.